A NONSENSE ANTHOLOGY

HE must be a fool indeed who cannot at times play the fool; and he who does not enjoy nonsense must be lacking in sense.

WILLIAM J. ROLFE.

A Nonsense Anthology

Collected by
Carolyn Wells

DOVER PUBLICATIONS, INC.

NEW YORK

PN
6110
N6
W4

Copyright © 1958 by Dover Publications, Inc.

This new Dover edition first published in 1958 is an unabridged republication of the first edition with a new index of first lines added.

Manufactured in the United States of America

Dover Publications, Inc.
180 Varick Street
New York 14, N. Y.

TO

GELETT BURGESS

A NONSENSE LOVER

CONTENTS

		PAGE
INTRODUCTION		xv

JABBERWOCKERY

JABBERWOCKY	Lewis Carroll	3
MORS IABROCHII	Anonymous	4
THE NYUM-NYUM	Anonymous	6
UFFIA	Harriet R. White	10
SPIRK TROLL-DERISIVE	James Whitcomb Riley	10
THE WHANGO TREE	1840	12
SING FOR THE GARISH EYE	W. S. Gilbert	13
THE CRUISE OF THE "P. C."	Anonymous	13
TO MARIE	Anonymous	14

ABSURD ASSOCIATIONS

LUNAR STANZAS	Henry Coggswell Knight	15
NONSENSE	Anonymous, 1617	16
SONNET FOUND IN A DESERTED MAD HOUSE	Anonymous	18
THE OCEAN WANDERER	Anonymous	18
SHE'S ALL MY FANCY PAINTED HIM	Lewis Carroll	20
MY RECOLLECTEST THOUGHTS	Charles E. Carryl	21
FATHER WILLIAM	Anonymous	22
IN THE GLOAMING	James C. Bayles	23
BALLAD OF BEDLAM	Punch	24
'T IS SWEET TO ROAM	Anonymous	25
HYMN TO THE SUNRISE	Anonymous	25

[vii]

Contents

		PAGE
THE MOON IS UP	Anonymous	26
'TIS MIDNIGHT	Anonymous	26
UPRISING SEE THE FITFUL LARK	Anonymous	27
LIKE TO THE THUNDERING TONE	Bishop Corbet	27
MY DREAM	Anonymous	28
MY HOME	Anonymous	29

"SERIOUS" SUBJECTS

IN IMMEMORIAM	Cuthbert Bede	29
THE HIGHER PANTHEISM IN A NUTSHELL	A. C. Swinburne	30
DARWINITY	Herman Merivale	31
SONG OF THE SCREW	Anonymous	33
MOORLANDS OF THE NOT	Anonymous	36
METAPHYSICS	Oliver Herford	36
ABSTROSOPHY	Gelett Burgess	37
ABSTEMIA	Gelett Burgess	38
PSYCHOLOPHON	Gelett Burgess	39
TIMON OF ARCHIMEDES	Charles Battell Loomis	39
ALONE	Anonymous	40
LINES BY A MEDIUM	Anonymous	41
TRANSCENDENTALISM	From the Times of India	41
INDIFFERENCE	Anonymous	42
QUATRAIN	Anonymous	43

HIGH SENTIMENTS

COSSIMBAZAR	Henry S. Leigh	43
THE PERSONIFIED SENTIMENTAL	Bret Harte	44
A CLASSIC ODE	Charles Battell Loomis	45
WHERE AVALANCHES WAIL	Anonymous	45
BLUE MOONSHINE	Francis G. Stokes	46

[viii]

Contents

		PAGE
NONSENSE	Thomas Moore	47
SUPERIOR NONSENSE VERSES	Anonymous	47
WHEN MOONLIKE ORE THE HAZURE SEAS	W. M. Thackeray	49
LINES BY A PERSON OF QUALITY	Alexander Pope	50
FRANGIPANNI	Anonymous	51
LINES BY A FOND LOVER	Anonymous	53
FORCING A WAY	Anonymous	54
THY HEART	Anonymous	55
A LOVE-SONG BY A LUNATIC	Anonymous	55
THE PARTERRE	E. H. Palmer	56
TO MOLLIDUSTA	Planché	57
JOHN JONES	A. C. Swinburne	57

SONGS AND BALLADS

THE OWL AND THE PUSSY-CAT	Edward Lear	59
A BALLADE OF THE NURSERIE	John Twig	60
A BALLAD OF HIGH ENDEAVOR	Anonymous	62
THE LUGUBRIOUS WHING-WHANG	James Whitcomb Riley	63
OH! WEARY MOTHER	Barry Pain	64
SWISS AIR	Bret Harte	64
THE BULBUL	Owen Seaman	65
BALLAD	Anonymous	65
OH, MY GERALDINE	F. C. Burnand	66

RESOUNDING TRIVIALITIES

BUZ, QUOTH THE BLUE FLY	Ben Jonson	66

[ix]

Contents

		PAGE
A Song on King William III	Anonymous	67
There was a Monkey	Anonymous, 1626	67
The Guinea Pig	Anonymous	68
Three Children	London, 1662	69
If	Anonymous	70
A Riddle	Anonymous	70
Three Jovial Huntsmen	Anonymous	70
Three Acres of Land	Anonymous	71
Master and Man	Anonymous	72
Hyder Iddle	Anonymous	73
King Arthur	Anonymous	73
In the Dumps	Anonymous	74
Tweedle-Dum and Tweedle-Dee	Anonymous	74
Martin to his Man	From Deuteromelia	74

NONSENSE BY LEAR

The Yonghy-Bonghy-Bó	Edward Lear	76
The Pobble who has no Toes	Edward Lear	81
The Jumblies	Edward Lear	83
Incidents in the Life of my Uncle Arly	Edward Lear	86
Lines to a Young Lady	Edward Lear	88

NONSENSE BY LEWIS CARROLL

Ways and Means	Lewis Carroll	90
The Walrus and the Carpenter	Lewis Carroll	93
The Hunting of the Snark	Lewis Carroll	97
Sylvie and Bruno	Lewis Carroll	101

[x]

Contents

		PAGE
INVOLVED PLOTS		
GENTLE ALICE BROWN	W. S. Gilbert	102
THE STORY OF PRINCE AGIB	W. S. Gilbert	107
FERDINANDO AND ELVIRA, OR THE GENTLE PIEMAN	W. S. Gilbert	110
GENERAL JOHN	W. S. Gilbert	112
NAUTICAL MISCELLANY		
LITTLE BILLEE	W. M. Thackeray	114
THE WRECK OF THE "JULIE PLANTE"	William H. Drummond	116
THE SHIPWRECK	E. H. Palmer	118
A SAILOR'S YARN	J. J. Roche	120
RIDICULOUS NARRATIVES		
THE WALLOPING WINDOW-BLIND	Charles E. Carryl	123
THE ROLLICKING MASTODON	Arthur Macy	125
THE SILVER QUESTION	Oliver Herford	127
THE SINGULAR SANGFROID OF BABY BUNTING	Guy Wetmore Carryl	129
FAITHLESS NELLY GRAY	Thomas Hood	131
THE ELDERLY GENTLEMAN	George Canning	134
MACARONIC VERSE		
MALUM OPUS	James Appleton Morgan	135
ÆSTIVATION	O. W. Holmes	136
A HOLIDAY TASK	Gilbert Abbott à Becket	137
PUER EX JERSEY	Anonymous	138
THE LITTLE PEACH	Anonymous	138
MONSIEUR MCGINTÉ	Anonymous	139

[xi]

Contents

AN ARCHAIC GESTE

		PAGE
YE LAYE OF YE WOODPECKORE	Henry A. Beers . . .	139

WEERD SPELINGS

COLLUSION BETWEEN A ALEGAITER AND A WATER-SNAIK . . .	J. W. Morris	143
ODD TO A KROKIS . .	Anonymous	146
SOME VERSES TO SNAIX .	Anonymous	147

ELEGIES, PAEONS, ODES

A GREAT MAN . . .	Oliver Goldsmith . . .	148
AN ELEGY	Oliver Goldsmith . . .	149
PARSON GRAY	Oliver Goldsmith . . .	150
AN ELEGY ON THE DEATH OF A MAD DOG . .	Oliver Goldsmith . . .	151
THE WONDERFUL OLD MAN	Anonymous	153
A CHRONICLE	Anonymous	155
ON THE OXFORD CARRIER	John Milton	157

PARODIES

NEPHELIDIA	A. C. Swinburne . .	158
MARTIN LUTHER AT POTSDAM	Barry Pain	160
COMPANIONS	C. S. Calverley . . .	163
THE COCK AND THE BULL	C. S. Calverley . . .	165
LOVERS AND A REFLECTION	C. S. Calverley . . .	170
AN IMITATION OF WORDSWORTH	Catharine M. Fanshawe .	173
THE FAMOUS BALLAD OF THE JUBILEE CUP . .	Arthur T. Quiller-Couch	175
A SONG OF IMPOSSIBILITIES	W. M. Praed . . .	183
TRUST IN WOMEN . .	Anonymous	186

[xii]

Contents

		PAGE
HERE IS THE TALE	Anthony C. Deane	188
THE AULD WIFE	C. S. Calverley	192
NOT I	R. L. Stevenson	194
MINNIE AND WINNIE	Lord Tennyson	194
THE MAYOR OF SCUTTLETON	Mary Mapes Dodge	195

QUATRAINS BY GELETT BURGESS

THE PURPLE COW	Gelett Burgess	196
THE INVISIBLE BRIDGE	Gelett Burgess	196
THE LAZY ROOF	Gelett Burgess	197
MY FEET	Gelett Burgess	197

ZANY ZOOLOGY

THE HEN	Oliver Herford	197
THE COW	Oliver Herford	198
THE CHIMPANZEE	Oliver Herford	199
THE HIPPOPOTAMUS	Oliver Herford	199
THE PLATYPUS	Oliver Herford	199
SOME GEESE	Oliver Herford	200
THE FLAMINGO	Lewis Gaylord Clark	201
KINDNESS TO ANIMALS	J. Ashby-Sterry	203
SAGE COUNSEL	A. T. Quiller-Couch	204
OF BAITING THE LION	Owen Seaman	205
THE FROG	Hilaire Belloc	207
THE YAK	Hilaire Belloc	207
THE PYTHON	Hilaire Belloc	208
THE BISON	Hilaire Belloc	209
THE PANTHER	Anonymous	209
THE MONKEY'S GLUE	Goldwin Goldsmith	210
THERE WAS A FROG	Christ Church MS.	211
THE BLOATED BIGGABOON	H. Cholmondeley-Pennell	211

PARADOXES, PARANOMASIAS AND WORD PLAYS

| WILD FLOWERS | Peter Newell | 212 |

[xiii]

Contents

		PAGE
TIMID HORTENSE	Peter Newell	212
HER POLKA DOTS	Peter Newell	212
HER DAIRY	Peter Newell	213
TURVEY TOP	Anonymous	213
WHAT THE PRINCE OF I DREAMT	H. Cholmondeley-Pennell	215

FOR CHILDREN

THE DINKEY-BIRD	Eugene Field	218
THE MAN IN THE MOON	James Whitcomb Riley	220
THE STORY OF THE WILD HUNTSMAN	Dr. Heinrich Hoffman	222

EGYPT AND THE ORIENT

THE STORY OF PYRAMID THOTHMES	Anonymous	224
THE STORY OF CRUEL PSAMTEK	Anonymous	225
THE CUMBERBUNCE	Paul West	226
THE AHKOND OF SWAT	Edward Lear	230
A THRENODY	George Thomas Lanigan	233
DIRGE OF THE MOOLLA OF KOTAL	George Thomas Lanigan	235

IMPOSSIBLE NAMES

RUSSIAN AND TURK	Anonymous	238
LINES TO MISS FLORENCE HUNTINGDON	Anonymous	239

IMPOSSIBILITIES

COBBE'S PROPHECIES	1614	241
AN UNSUSPECTED FACT	Edward Cannon	242

PERSONALITIES

THE SORROWS OF WERTHER	W. M. Thackeray	242
NONSENSE VERSES	Charles Lamb	243
THE NOBLE TUCK-MAN	Jean Ingelow	244
THE PESSIMIST	Ben King	245

Contents

		PAGE
THE MODERN HIAWATHA	Anonymous	246
ON THE ROAD	Tudor Jenks	247
UNCLE SIMON AND UNCLE JIM	Artemus Ward	247
POOR DEAR GRANDPAPA	D'Arcy W. Thompson	247
THE SEA-SERPENT	Planché	248
MELANCHOLIA	Anonymous	248
THE MONKEY'S WEDDING	Anonymous	248
MR. FINNEY'S TURNIP	Anonymous	250

QUATRAINS

THE SUN	J. Davis	251
THE AUTUMN LEAVES	Anonymous	251
IN THE NIGHT	Anonymous	251
POOR BROTHER	Anonymous	251
THE BOY	Eugene Field	252
THE SEA	Anonymous	252

RUTHLESS RHYMES

THERE WAS A LITTLE GIRL	H. W. Longfellow	253
FIN DE SIÈCLE	Newton Mackintosh	253
MARY JANE	Anonymous	253
TENDER-HEARTEDNESS	Col. D. Streamer	253
IMPETUOUS SAMUEL	Col. D. Streamer	254
MISFORTUNES NEVER COME SINGLY	Col. D. Streamer	254
AUNT ELIZA	Col. D. Streamer	254
SUSAN	Anonymous	254
BABY AND MARY	Anonymous	255
THE SUNBEAM	Anonymous	255
LITTLE WILLIE	Anonymous	255
MARY AMES	Anonymous	256

MALAPROPISMS, THIEVES CANT, AND JARGON

MUDDLED METAPHORS	Tom Hood, Jr.	256
VILLON'S STRAIGHT TIP TO ALL CROSS COVES	W. E. Henley	257

[xv]

Contents

		PAGE
ODE TO THE HUMAN HEART	Laman Blanchard	258

LIMERICKS

LIMERICKS	Edward Lear	260
	Anonymous . . .	262
	Cosmo Monkhouse . .	263
	Walter Parke	264
	George du Maurier . .	265
	Robert J. Burdette . .	266
	Gelett Burgess . . .	266
	Bruce Porter	267
	Newton Mackintosh . .	267
	Anonymous . . .	267
	Anonymous . . .	268
	Anonymous . . .	268

INTRODUCTION

INTRODUCTION

ON a topographical map of Literature Nonsense would be represented by a small and sparsely settled country, neglected by the average tourist, but affording keen delight to the few enlightened travellers who sojourn within its borders. It is a field which has been neglected by anthologists and essayists; one of its few serious recognitions being in a certain "Treatise of Figurative Language," which says: "Nonsense; shall we dignify that with a place on our list? Assuredly will vote for doing so every one who hath at all duly noticed what admirable and wise uses it can be, and often is, put to, though never before in rhetoric has it been so highly honored. How deeply does clever or quaint nonsense abide in the memory, and for how many a decade — from earliest youth to age's most venerable years."

And yet Hazlitt's "Studies in Jocular Literature" mentions six divisions of the Jest, and omits Nonsense!

Perhaps, partly because of such neglect, the work of the best nonsense writers is less widely known than it might be.

But a more probable reason is that the majority of the reading world does not appreciate or enjoy real nonsense, and this, again, is consequent upon their inability to discriminate between nonsense of integral merit and simple chaff.

> A jest's prosperity lies in the ear
> Of him that hears it. Never in the tongue
> Of him that makes it,

and a sense of nonsense is as distinct a part of our mentality as a sense of humor, being by no means identical therewith.

It is a fad at present for a man to relate a nonsensical story, and then, if his hearer does not laugh, say gravely: "You have no sense of humor. That is a test story, and only a true humorist laughs at it." Now, the hearer may have an exquisite sense of humor, but he may be lacking in a sense of nonsense, and so the story gives him no pleasure. De Quincey said, "None but a man of extraordinary talent can write first-rate nonsense." Only a short study of the subject is required to convince us that De Quincey was right; and he might have added, none but a man of extraordinary taste can appreciate first-rate nonsense. As an instance of this, we may remember that Edward Lear, "the parent of modern nonsense-writers," was a talented author and artist, and a prime favorite of such men as Tennyson and the Earls of

Introduction

Derby; and John Ruskin placed Lear's name at the head of his list of the best hundred authors.

"Don't tell me," said William Pitt, "of a man's being able to talk sense; every one can talk sense. Can he talk nonsense?"

The sense of nonsense enables us not only to discern pure nonsense, but to consider intelligently nonsense of various degrees of purity. Absence of sense is not necessarily nonsense, any more than absence of justice is injustice.

Etymologically speaking, nonsense may be either words without meaning, or words conveying absurd or ridiculous ideas. It is the second definition which expresses the great mass of nonsense literature, but there is a small proportion of written nonsense which comes under the head of language without meaning.

Again, there are verses composed entirely of meaningless words, which are not nonsense literature, because they are written with some other intent.

The nursery rhyme, of which there are almost as many versions as there are nurseries,

> Eena, meena, mona, mi,
> Bassalona, bona, stri,
> Hare, ware, frown, whack,
> Halico balico, we, wi, wo, wack,

is not strictly a nonsense verse, because it was invented and used for "counting out," and the arbitrary words simply take the place of the numbers 1, 2, 3, etc.

Also, the nonsense verses with which students of Latin composition are sometimes taught to begin their efforts, where words are used with no relative meaning, simply to familiarize the pupil with the mechanical values of quantity and metre, are not nonsense. It is only nonsense for nonsense' sake that is now under our consideration.

Doubtless the best and best-known example of versified words without meaning is "Jabberwocky." Although (notwithstanding Lewis Carroll's explanations) the coined words are absolutely without meaning, the rhythm is perfect and the poetic quality decidedly apparent, and the poem appeals to the nonsense lover as a work of pure genius. Bayard Taylor is said to have recited "Jabberwocky" aloud for his own delectation until he was forced to stop by uncontrollable laughter. To us who know our *Alice* it would seem unnecessary to quote this poem, but it is a fact that among the general reading community the appreciators of Lewis Carroll are surprisingly few. An editor of a leading literary review, when asked recently if he had read "Alice in Wonderland," replied, "No, but I mean to. It is by the author of 'As in a Looking-Glass,' is it not?"

Introduction

But of far greater interest and merit than nonsense of words, is nonsense of ideas. Here, again, we distinguish between nonsense and no sense. Ideas conveying no sense are often intensely funny, and this type is seen in some of the best of our nonsense literature.

A perfect specimen is the bit of evidence read by the White Rabbit at the Trial of the Knave of Hearts.[1] One charm of these verses is the serious air of legal directness which pervades their ambiguity, and another is the precision with which the metrical accent coincides exactly with the natural emphasis. They are marked, too, by the liquid euphony that always distinguishes Lewis Carroll's poetry.

A different type is found in verses that refer to objects in terms the opposite of true, thereby suggesting ludicrous incongruity, and there is also the nonsense verse that uses word effects which have been confiscated by the poets and tacitly given over to them.

A refrain of nonsense words is a favorite diversion of many otherwise serious poets.

With a hey, and a ho, and a hey nonino,

is one of Shakespeare's many musical nonsense refrains.

[1] "She's all my Fancy painted him," page 20.

Burns gives us:

> Ken ye aught o' Captain Grose?
> Igo and ago,
> If he's 'mang his freens or foes?
> Iram, coram, dago.
> Is he slain by Highlan' bodies?
> Igo and ago;
> And eaten like a weather haggis?
> Iram, coram, dago.

Another very old refrain runs thus:

> Rorum, corum, sunt di-vorum,
> Harum, scarum, divo;
> Tag-rag, merry-derry, periwig and hat-band,
> Hic, hoc, horum, genitivo.

An old ballad written before the Reformation has for a refrain:

> Sing go trix,
> Trim go trix,
> Under the greenwood tree.

While a celebrated political ballad is known by its nonsense chorus,

> Lilliburlero bullin a-la.

Mother Goose rhymes abound in these nonsense refrains, and they are often fine examples of onomatopœia.

By far the most meritorious and most interesting kind of nonsense is that which embodies an absurd

Introduction

or ridiculous idea, and treats it with elaborate seriousness. The greatest masters of this art are undoubtedly Edward Lear and Lewis Carroll. These Englishmen were men of genius, deep thinkers, and hard workers.

Lear was an artist draughtsman, his subjects being mainly ornithological and zoölogical. Lewis Carroll (Charles L. Dodgson) was an expert in mathematics and a lecturer on that science in Christ Church, Oxford.

Both these men numbered among their friends many of the greatest Englishmen of the day. Tennyson was a warm friend and admirer of each, as was also John Ruskin.

Lear's first nonsense verses, published in 1846, are written in the form of the well-known stanza beginning:

> There was an old man of Tobago.

This type of stanza, known as the "Limerick," is said by a gentleman who speaks with authority to have flourished in the reign of William IV. This is one of several he remembers as current at his public school in 1834:

> There was a young man at St. Kitts
> Who was very much troubled with fits;
>   The eclipse of the moon
>   Threw him into a swoon,
> When he tumbled and broke into bits.

Lear distinctly asserts that this form of verse was not invented by him, but was suggested by a friend as a useful model for amusing rhymes. It proved so in his case, for he published no less than two hundred and twelve of these "Limericks."

In regard to his verses, Lear asserted that "nonsense, pure and absolute," was his aim throughout; and remarked, further, that to have been the means of administering innocent mirth to thousands was surely a just excuse for satisfaction. He pursued his aim with scrupulous consistency, and his absurd conceits are fantastic and ridiculous, but never cheaply or vulgarly funny.

Twenty-five years after his first book came out, Lear published other books of nonsense verse and prose, with pictures which are irresistibly mirth-provoking. Lear's nonsense songs, while retaining all the ludicrous merriment of his Limericks, have an added quality of poetic harmony. They are distinctly *singable*, and many of them have been set to music by talented composers. Perhaps the best-known songs are "The Owl and the Pussy-Cat" and "The Daddy-Long-Legs and the Fly."

Lear himself composed airs for "The Pelican Chorus" and "The Yonghy-Bonghy Bò," which were arranged for the piano by Professor Pomè, of San Remo, Italy.

Introduction

Although like Lear's in some respects, Lewis Carroll's nonsense is perhaps of a more refined type. There is less of the grotesque and more poetic imagery. But though Carroll was more of a poet than Lear, both had the true sense of nonsense. Both assumed the most absurd conditions, and proceeded to detail their consequences with a simple seriousness that convulses appreciative readers, and we find ourselves uncertain whether it is the manner or the matter that is more amusing.

Lewis Carroll was a man of intellect and education; his funniest sayings are often based on profound knowledge or deep thought. Like Lear, he never spoiled his quaint fancies by over-exaggerating their quaintness or their fancifulness, and his ridiculous plots are as carefully conceived, constructed, and elaborated as though they embodied the soundest facts. No funny detail is ever allowed to become *too* funny; and it is in this judicious economy of extravagance that his genius is shown. As he remarks in one of his own poems:

> Then, fourthly, there are epithets
> That suit with any word —
> As well as Harvey's Reading Sauce
> With fish, or flesh, or bird.
>
> . . . . . .

> Such epithets, like pepper,
>   Give zest to what you write;
> And, if you strew them sparely,
>   They whet the appetite;
> But if you lay them on too thick,
>   You spoil the matter quite!

Both Lear and Carroll suffered from the undiscerning critics who persisted in seeing in their nonsense a hidden meaning, a cynical, political, or other intent, veiled under the apparent foolery. Lear takes occasion to deny this in the preface to one of his books, and asserts not only that his rhymes and pictures have no symbolical meaning, but that he "took more care than might be supposed to make the subjects incapable of such misinterpretation."

Likewise, "Jabberwocky" was declared by one critic to be a translation from the German, and by others its originality was doubted. The truth is, that it was written by Lewis Carroll at an evening party; it was quite impromptu, and no ulterior meaning was intended. "The Hunting of the Snark" was also regarded by some as an allegory, or, perhaps, a burlesque on a celebrated case, in which the *Snark* was used as a personification of popularity, but Lewis Carroll protested that the poem had no meaning at all.

A favorite trick of the Nonsensists is the coining

Introduction

of words to suit their needs, and Lear and Carroll are especially happy in their inventions of this kind.

Lear gives us such gems as scroobious, meloobious, ombliferous, borascible, slobaciously, himmeltanious, flumpetty, and mumbian; while the best of Lewis Carroll's coined words are those found in "Jabberwocky."

Another of the great Nonsensists is W. S. Gilbert. Unlike Lear or Carroll, his work is not characterized by absurd words or phrases; he prefers a still wider scope, and invents a ridiculous plot. The "Bab Ballads," as well as Mr. Gilbert's comic opera librettos, hinge upon schemes of ludicrous impossibility, which are treated as the most natural proceedings in the world. The best known of the "Bab Ballads" is no doubt "The Yarn of the 'Nancy Bell,'" which was long since set to music and is still a popular song. In addition to his talent for nonsense, Mr. Gilbert possesses a wonderful rhyming facility, and juggles cleverly with difficult and unusual metres.

In regard to his "Bab Ballads," Mr. Gilbert gravely says that "they are not, as a rule, founded on fact," and, remembering their gory and often cannibalistic tendencies, we are grateful for this assurance. An instance of Gilbert's appreciation of other people's nonsense is his parody of Lear's verse:

> There was an old man in a tree
> Who was horribly bored by a bee;
> When they said, "Does it buzz?"
> He replied, "Yes, it does!
> It's a regular brute of a bee!"

The parody attributed to Gilbert is called "A Nonsense Rhyme in Blank Verse":

> There was an old man of St. Bees,
> Who was stung in the arm by a wasp;
> When they asked, "Does it hurt?"
> He replied, "No, it does n't,
> But I thought all the while 't was a Hornet!"

Thackeray wrote spirited nonsense, but much of it had an under-meaning, political or otherwise, which bars it from the field of sheer nonsense.

The sense of nonsense is no respecter of persons; even staid old Dr. Johnson possessed it, though his nonsense verses are marked by credible fact and irrefutable logic. Witness these two examples:

> As with my hat upon my head
> I walked along the Strand,
> I there did meet another man
> With his hat in his hand.

> The tender infant, meek and mild,
> Fell down upon the stone;
> The nurse took up the squealing child,
> But still the child squealed on.

Introduction

The Doctor is also responsible for

> If a man who turnips cries,
> Cry not when his father dies,
> 'T is a proof that he would rather
> Have a turnip than a father.

And indeed, among our best writers there are few who have not dropped into nonsense or semi-nonsense at one time or another.

A familiar bit of nonsense prose is by S. Foote, and it is said that Charles Macklin used to recite it with great gusto:

"She went into the garden to cut a cabbage-leaf to make an apple-pie, and at the same time a great she-bear coming up the street, pops its head into the shop. 'What, no soap?' so he died. She imprudently married the barber, and there were present the Pickaninnies, the Joblilies, the Gayrulies, and the Grand Panjandrum himself with the little round button on top, and they all fell to playing catch-as-catch-can till the gunpowder ran out at the heels of their boots."

An old nonsense verse attributed to an Oxford student, is the well known

> A centipede was happy quite,
>   Until a frog in fun
> Said, "Pray, which leg comes after which?"
> This raised her mind to such a pitch,
>   She lay distracted in the ditch
>   Considering how to run.

So far as we know, Kipling has never printed

anything which can be called nonsense verse, but it is doubtless only a question of time when that branch shall be added to his versatility. His "Just So" stories are capital nonsense prose, and the following rhyme proves him guilty of at least one Limerick:

> There was a small boy of Quebec,
> Who was buried in snow to his neck;
>   When they said, "Are you friz?"
>   He replied, "Yes, I is —
> But we don't call this cold in Quebec."

Among living authors, one who has written a great amount of good nonsense is Mr. Gelett Burgess, late editor of *The Lark*.

According to Mr. Burgess' own statement, the test of nonsense is its quotability, and his work stands this test admirably, for what absurd rhyme ever attained such popularity as his "Purple Cow"? This was first printed in *The Lark*, a paper published in San Francisco for two years, the only periodical of any merit that has ever made intelligent nonsense its special feature.

Another of the most talented nonsense writers of to-day is Mr. Oliver Herford. It is a pity, however, to reproduce his verse without his illustrations, for as nonsense these are as admirable as the text. But the greater part of Mr. Herford's work belongs to the realm of pure fancy, and though of a whimsical delicacy often equal to Lewis Carroll's, it is rarely sheer nonsense.

As a proof that good nonsense is by no means an easy achievement, attention is called to a recent competition inaugurated by the London *Academy*.

Nonsense rhymes similar to those quoted from *The Lark* were asked for, and though many were received, it is stated that no brilliant results were among them.

The prize was awarded to this weak and uninteresting specimen:

> " If half the road was made of jam,
>   The other half of bread,
> How very nice my walks would be,"
>   The greedy infant said.

These two were also offered by competitors:

> I love to stand upon my head
>   And think of things sublime
> Until my mother interrupts
>   And says it's dinner-time.

> A lobster wooed a lady crab,
>   And kissed her lovely face.
> " Upon my sole," the crabbess cried,
>   " I wish you 'd mind your plaice ! "

Let us, then, give Nonsense its place among the divisions of Humor, and though we cannot reduce it to an exact science, let us acknowledge it as a fine art.

A NONSENSE ANTHOLOGY

A Nonsense Anthology

JABBERWOCKY

'TWAS brillig, and the slithy toves
    Did gyre and gimble in the wabe;
    All mimsy were the borogoves,
And the mome raths outgrabe.

" Beware the Jabberwock, my son !
    The jaws that bite, the claws that catch !
Beware the Jubjub bird, and shun
    The frumious Bandersnatch ! "

He took his vorpal sword in hand :
    Long time the manxome foe he sought.
So rested he by the Tumtum tree,
    And stood awhile in thought.

And as in uffish thought he stood,
    The Jabberwock with eyes of flame,
Came whiffling through the tulgey wood,
    And burbled as it came !

One, two ! One, two ! And through, and through
    The vorpal blade went snicker-snack !
He left it dead, and with its head
    He went galumphing back.

"And hast thou slain the Jabberwock?
  Come to my arms, my beamish boy!
Oh, frabjous day! Callooh! callay!"
  He chortled in his joy.

'T was brillig, and the slithy toves
  Did gyre and gimble in the wabe;
All mimsy were the borogoves
  And the mome raths outgrabe.

Lewis Carroll.

MORS IABROCHII

Cœsper[1] erat: tunc lubriciles[2] ultravia circum
  Urgebant gyros gimbiculosque tophi;
Mœstenui visæ borogovides ire meatu;
  Et profugi gemitus exgrabuêre rathæ.

O fuge Iabrochium, sanguis meus![3] Ille recurvis
  Unguibus, estque avidis dentibus ille minax.
Ububæ fuge cautus avis vim, gnate! Neque unquam
  Fæderpax contra te frumiosus eat!

---

[1] *Cœsper* from *Cœna* and *vesper*.
[2] *lubriciles* from *lubricus* and *graciles*. See the Commentary in Humpty Dumpty's square, which will also explain *ultravia*, and — if it requires explanation — *mœstenui*.
[3] *Sanguis meus*: cf. Verg. Æn. 6. 836,
  "Projice tela manu, sanguis meus!"

A Nonsense Anthology

Vorpali gladio juvenis succingitur : hostis
  Manxumus ad medium quæritur usque diem :
Jamque viâ fesso, sed plurima mente prementi,
  Tumtumiæ frondis suaserat umbra moram.

Consilia interdum stetit egnia [1] mene revolvens ;
  At gravis in densâ fronde susuffrus [2] erat,
Spiculaque [3] ex oculis jacientis flammea, tulseam
  Per silvam venit burbur [4] Iabrochii !

Vorpali, semel atque iterum collectus in ictum,
  Persnicuit gladis persnacuitque puer :
Deinde galumphatus, spernens informe Cadaver,
  Horrendum monstri rettulit ipse caput.

Victor Iabrochii, spoliis insignis opimis,
  Rursus in amplexus, o radiose, meos !
O frabiose dies ! CALLO clamateque CALLA !
  Vix potuit lætus chorticulare pater.

Cœsper erat : tunc lubriciles ultravia circum
  Urgebant gyros gimbiculosque tophi ;
Mœstenui visæ borogovides ire meatu ;
  Et profugi gemitus exgrabuêre rathæ.

Anonymous.

---

[1] *egnia :* " muffish "= segnis ; ... " uffish "= egnis. This is a conjectural analogy, but I can suggest no better solution.
[2] *susuffrus :* " whiffling " : : *susurrus :* " whistling."
[3] *spicula :* see the picture.
[4] *burbur :* apparently a labial variation of *murmur*, stronger but more dissonant.

[5]

THE NYUM-NYUM

THE Nyum-Nyum chortled by the sea,
    And sipped the wavelets green:
    He wondered how the sky could be
So very nice and clean;

He wondered if the chambermaid
    Had swept the dust away,
And if the scrumptious Jabberwock
    Had mopped it up that day.

And then in sadness to his love
    The Nyum-Nyum weeping said,
I know no reason why the sea
    Should not be white or red.

I know no reason why the sea
    Should not be red, I say;
And why the slithy Bandersnatch
    Has not been round to-day.

He swore he'd call at two o'clock,
    And now it's half-past four.
"Stay," said the Nyum-Nyum's love, "I think
    I hear him at the door."

In twenty minutes in there came
    A creature black as ink,
Which put its feet upon a chair
    And called for beer to drink.

They gave him porter in a tub,
　　But, "Give me more!" he cried;
And then he drew a heavy sigh,
　　And laid him down, and died.

He died, and in the Nyum-Nyum's cave
　　A cry of mourning rose;
The Nyum-Nyum sobbed a gentle sob,
　　And slily blew his nose.

The Nyum-Nyum's love, we need not state,
　　Was overwhelmed and sad;
She said, "Oh, take the corpse away,
　　Or you will drive me mad!"

The Nyum-Nyum in his supple arms
　　Took up the gruesome weight,
And, with a cry of bitter fear,
　　He threw it at his mate.

And then he wept, and tore his hair,
　　And threw it in the sea,
And loudly sobbed with streaming eyes
　　That such a thing could be.

The ox, that mumbled in his stall,
　　Perspired and gently sighed,
And then, in sympathy, it fell
　　Upon its back and died.

The hen that sat upon her eggs,
  With high ambition fired,
Arose in simple majesty,
  And, with a cluck, expired.

The jubejube bird, that carolled there,
  Sat down upon a post,
And with a reverential caw,
  Gave up its little ghost.

And ere its kind and loving life
  Eternally had ceased,
The donkey, in the ancient barn,
  In agony deceased.

The raven, perched upon the elm,
  Gave forth a scraping note,
And ere the sound had died away,
  Had cut its tuneful throat.

The Nyum-Nyum's love was sorrowful;
  And, after she had cried,
She, with a brand-new carving-knife,
  Committed suicide.

"Alas!" the Nyum-Nyum said, "alas!
  With thee I will not part,"
And straightway seized a rolling-pin
  And drove it through his heart.

The mourners came and gathered up
   The bits that lay about;
But why the massacre had been,
   They could not quite make out.

One said there was a mystery
   Connected with the deaths;
But others thought the silent ones
   Perhaps had lost their breaths.

The doctor soon arrived, and viewed
   The corpses as they lay;
He could not give them life again,
   So he was heard to say.

But, oh! it was a horrid sight;
   It made the blood run cold,
To see the bodies carried off
   And covered up with mould.

The Toves across the briny sea
   Wept buckets-full of tears;
They were relations of the dead,
   And had been friends for years.

The Jabberwock upon the hill
   Gave forth a gloomy wail,
When in his airy seat he sat,
   And told the awful tale.

And who can wonder that it made
  That loving creature cry?
For he had done the dreadful work
  And caused the things to die.

That Jabberwock was passing bad —
  That Jabberwock was wrong,
And with this verdict I conclude
  One portion of my song.

Anonymous.

UFFIA

WHEN sporgles spanned the floreate mead
    And cogwogs gleet upon the lea,
  Uffia gopped to meet her love
Who smeeged upon the equat sea.

Dately she walked aglost the sand;
  The boreal wind seet in her face;
The moggling waves yalped at her feet;
  Pangwangling was her pace.

Harriet R. White.

SPIRK TROLL–DERISIVE*

THE Crankadox leaned o'er the edge of the moon,
  And wistfully gazed on the sea
Where the Gryxabodill madly whistled a tune
  To the air of "Ti-fol-de-ding-dee."

* By permission of the author; from "Spirk and Wunk Rhymes," copyright, 1891, 1898.

The quavering shriek of the Fliupthecreek
  Was fitfully wafted afar
To the Queen of the Wunks as she powdered her cheek
  With the pulverized rays of a star.

The Gool closed his ear on the voice of the Grig,
  And his heart it grew heavy as lead
As he marked the Baldekin adjusting his wig
  On the opposite side of his head;
And the air it grew chill as the Gryxabodill
  Raised his dank, dripping fins to the skies
To plead with the Plunk for the use of her bill
  To pick the tears out of his eyes.

The ghost of the Zhack flitted by in a trance;
  And the Squidjum hid under a tub
As he heard the loud hooves of the Hooken advance
  With a rub-a-dub-dub-a-dub dub!
And the Crankadox cried as he laid down and died,
  "My fate there is none to bewail!"
While the Queen of the Wunks drifted over the tide
  With a long piece of crape to her tail.

James Whitcomb Riley.

THE WHANGO TREE

THE woggly bird sat on the whango tree,
    Nooping the rinkum corn,
  And graper and graper, alas! grew he,
  And cursed the day he was born.
His crute was clum and his voice was rum,
  As curiously thus sang he,
"Oh, would I'd been rammed and eternally clammed
  Ere I perched on this whango tree."

Now the whango tree had a bubbly thorn,
  As sharp as a nootie's bill,
And it stuck in the woggly bird's umptum lorn
  And weepadge, the smart did thrill.
He fumbled and cursed, but that was n't the worst,
  For he could n't at all get free,
And he cried, "I am gammed, and injustibly nammed
  On the luggardly whango tree."

And there he sits still, with no worm in his bill,
  Nor no guggledom in his nest;
He is hungry and bare, and gobliddered with care,
  And his grabbles give him no rest;
He is weary and sore and his tugmut is soar,
  And nothing to nob has he,
As he chirps, "I am blammed and corruptibly jammed,
  In this cuggerdom whango tree."

1840.

SING FOR THE GARISH EYE

SING for the garish eye,
    When moonless brandlings cling!
  Let the froddering crooner cry,
And the braddled sapster sing.
For never and never again,
  Will the tottering beechlings play,
For bratticed wrackers are singing aloud,
  And the throngers croon in May!

W. S. Gilbert.

THE CRUISE OF THE "P. C."

ACROSS the swiffling waves they went,
    The gumly bark yoked to and fro;
  The jupple crew on pleasure bent,
Galored, "This is a go!"

Beside the poo's'l stood the Gom,
  He chirked and murgled in his glee;
While near him, in a grue jipon,
  The Bard was quite at sea.

"Gollop! Golloy! Thou scrumjous Bard!
  Take pen (thy stylo) and endite
A pome, my brain needs kurgling hard,
  And I will feast tonight."

That wansome Bard he took his pen,
   A flirgly look around he guv;
He squoffled once, he squirled, and then
   He wrote what's writ above.

Anonymous.

TO MARIE

WHEN the breeze from the bluebottle's blustering blim
   Twirls the toads in a tooroomaloo,
And the whiskery whine of the wheedlesome whim
   Drowns the roll of the rattatattoo,
Then I dream in the shade of the shally-go-shee,
   And the voice of the bally-molay
Brings the smell of the pale poppy-cod's blummered blee
   From the willy-wad over the way.

Ah, the shuddering shoe and the blinketty-blanks
   When the punglung falls from the bough
In the blast of a hurricane's hicketty-hanks
   O'er the hills of the hocketty-how!
Give the rigamarole to the clangery-whang,
   If they care for such fiddlededee;
But the thingumbob kiss of the whangery-bang
   Keeps the higgledy-piggle for me.

L'Envoi

It is pilly-po-doddle and aligobung
  When the lollypup covers the ground,
Yet the poldiddle perishes plunkety-pung
  When the heart jimny-coggles around.
If the soul cannot snoop at the gigglesome cart
  Seeking surcease in gluggety-glug,
It is useless to say to the pulsating heart,
  "Yankee-doodle ker-chuggety-chug!"

Anonymous.

LUNAR STANZAS

NIGHT saw the crew like pedlers with their packs
  Altho' it were too dear to pay for eggs;
Walk crank along with coffin on their backs
  While in their arms they bow their weary legs.

And yet 't was strange, and scarce can one suppose
  That a brown buzzard-fly should steal and wear
His white jean breeches and black woollen hose,
  But thence that flies have souls is very clear.

But, Holy Father! what shall save the soul,
  When cobblers ask three dollars for their shoes?
When cooks their biscuits with a shot-tower roll,
  And farmers rake their hay-cocks with their hoes.

Yet, 'twere profuse to see for pendant light,
    A tea-pot dangle in a lady's ear;
And 'twere indelicate, although she might
    Swallow two whales and yet the moon shine clear.

But what to me are woven clouds, or what,
    If dames from spiders learn to warp their looms?
If coal-black ghosts turn soldiers for the State,
    With wooden eyes, and lightning-rods for plumes?

Oh! too, too shocking! barbarous, savage taste!
    To eat one's mother ere itself was born!
To gripe the tall town-steeple by the waste,
    And scoop it out to be his drinking-horn.

No more: no more! I'm sick and dead and gone;
    Boxed in a coffin, stifled six feet deep;
Thorns, fat and fearless, prick my skin and bone,
    And revel o'er me, like a soulless sheep.

                    Henry Coggswell Knight, 1815.

NONSENSE

OH that my Lungs could bleat like butter'd Pease;
    But bleating of my lungs hath Caught the itch,
And are as mangy as the Irish Seas
    That offer wary windmills to the Rich.

I grant that Rainbowes being lull'd asleep,
  Snort like a woodknife in a Lady's eyes;
Which makes her grieve to see a pudding creep,
  For Creeping puddings only please the wise.

Not that a hard-row'd herring should presume
  To swing a tyth pig in a Cateskin purse;
For fear the hailstons which did fall at Rome,
  By lesning of the fault should make it worse.

For 't is most certain Winter woolsacks grow
  From geese to swans if men could keep them so,
Till that the sheep shorn Planets gave the hint
  To pickle pancakes in Geneva print.

Some men there were that did suppose the skie
  Was made of Carbonado'd Antidotes;
But my opinion is, a Whale's left eye,
  Need not be coynéd all King Harry groates.

The reason's plain, for Charon's Westerne barge
  Running a tilt at the Subjunctive mood,
Beckoned to Bednal Green, and gave him charge
  To fasten padlockes with Antartic food.

The End will be the Mill ponds must be laded,
  To fish for white pots in a Country dance;
So they that suffered wrong and were upbraded
  Shall be made friends in a left-handed trance.

                              Anonymous, 1617.

SONNET FOUND IN A DESERTED MAD HOUSE

OH that my soul a marrow-bone might seize!
   For the old egg of my desire is broken,
   Spilled is the pearly white and spilled the yolk, and
As the mild melancholy contents grease
My path the shorn lamb baas like bumblebees.
Time's trashy purse is as a taken token
Or like a thrilling recitation, spoken
By mournful mouths filled full of mirth and cheese.

And yet, why should I clasp the earthful urn?
Or find the frittered fig that felt the fast?
Or choose to chase the cheese around the churn?
Or swallow any pill from out the past?
Ah, no Love, not while your hot kisses burn
Like a potato riding on the blast.

Anonymous.

THE OCEAN WANDERER

BRIGHT breaks the warrior o'er the ocean wave
   Through realms that rove not, clouds that cannot save,
Sinks in the sunshine; dazzles o'er the tomb
And mocks the mutiny of Memory's gloom.

Oh! who can feel the crimson ecstasy
That soothes with bickering jar the Glorious
  Tree?
O'er the high rock the foam of gladness throws,
While star-beams lull Vesuvius to repose:
Girds the white spray, and in the blue lagoon,
Weeps like a walrus o'er the waning moon?
Who can declare? — not thou, pervading boy
Whom pibrochs pierce not, crystals cannot cloy; —
Not thou soft Architect of silvery gleams,
Whose soul would simmer in Hesperian streams,
Th' exhaustless fire — the bosom's azure bliss,
That hurtles, life-like, o'er a scene like this; —
Defies the distant agony of Day —
And sweeps o'er hetacombs — away! away!
Say shall Destruction's lava load the gale,
The furnace quiver and the mountain quail?
Say shall the son of Sympathy pretend
His cedar fragrance with our Chief's to blend?
There, where the gnarled monuments of sand
Howl their dark whirlwinds to the levin brand;
Conclusive tenderness; fraternal grog,
Tidy conjunction; adamantine bog,
Impetuous arrant toadstool; Thundering quince,
Repentant dog-star, inessential Prince,
Expound. Pre-Adamite eventful gun,
Crush retribution, currant-jelly, pun,
Oh! eligible Darkness, fender, sting,
Heav'n-born Insanity, courageous thing.
Intending, bending, scouring, piercing all,
Death like pomatum, tea, and crabs must fall.
                                    Anonymous.

SHE'S ALL MY FANCY PAINTED HIM

SHE's all my fancy painted him,
   (I make no idle boast);
If he or you had lost a limb,
   Which would have suffered most?

He said that you had been to her,
   And seen me here before:
But, in another character
   She was the same of yore.

There was not one that spoke to us,
   Of all that thronged the street;
So he sadly got into a 'bus,
   And pattered with his feet.

They told me you had been to her,
   And mentioned me to him;
She gave me a good character,
   But said I could not swim.

He sent them word I had not gone
   (We know it to be true);
If she should push the matter on,
   What would become of you?

I gave her one, they gave him two,
    You gave us three or more;
They all returned from him to you,
    Though they were mine before.

If I or she should chance to be
    Involved in this affair,
He trusts to you to set them free,
    Exactly as we were.

My notion was that you had been
    (Before she had this fit)
An obstacle that came between
    Him, and ourselves, and it.

Don't let him know she liked them best,
    For this must ever be
A secret, kept from all the rest,
    Between yourself and me.

Lewis Carroll.

MY RECOLLECTEST THOUGHTS*

My recollectest thoughts are those
    Which I remember yet;
And bearing on, as you'd suppose,
The things I don't forget.

---

* By permission of the author; from "Davy and the Goblin," copyright, 1884, 1885, by The Century Co.; 1885, by Ticknor & Co.

But my resemblest thoughts are less
    Alike than they should be;
A state of things, as you'll confess,
    You very seldom see.

And yet the mostest thought I love
    Is what no one believes —
That I'm the sole survivor of
    The famous Forty Thieves!

Charles E. Carryl.

FATHER WILLIAM

"YOU are old, Father William," the young man said,
    "And your nose has a look of surprise;
Your eyes have turned round to the back of your head,
    And you live upon cucumber pies."
"I know it, I know it," the old man replied,
    "And it comes from employing a quack,
Who said if I laughed when the crocodile died
    I should never have pains in my back."

"You are old, Father William," the young man said,
    "And your legs always get in your way;
You use too much mortar in mixing your bread,
    And you try to drink timothy hay."

"Very true, very true," said the wretched old man,
  "Every word that you tell me is true;
And it's caused by my having my kerosene can
  Painted red where it ought to be blue."

"You are old, Father William," the young man said,
  "And your teeth are beginning to freeze,
Your favorite daughter has wheels in her head,
  And the chickens are eating your knees."
"You are right," said the old man, "I cannot deny,
  That my troubles are many and great,
But I'll butter my ears on the Fourth of July,
  And then I'll be able to skate."

Anonymous.

IN THE GLOAMING

THE twilight twiles in the vernal vale,
  In adumbration of azure awe,
  And I listlessly list in my swallow-tail
To the limpet licking his limber jaw.
And it's O for the sound of the daffodil,
  For the dry distillings of prawn and prout,
When hope hops high and a heather hill
  Is a dear delight and a darksome doubt.
The snagwap sits in the bosky brae
  And sings to the gumplet in accents sweet;
The gibwink has n't a word to say,
  But pensively smiles at the fair keeweet.

And it's O for the jungles of Boorabul.
   For the jingling jungles to jangle in,
With a moony maze of mellado mull,
   And a protoplasm for next of kin.
O, sweet is the note of the shagreen shard
   And mellow the mew of the mastodon,
When the soboliferous Somminard
   Is scenting the shadows at set of sun.
And it's O for the timorous tamarind
   In the murky meadows of Mariboo,
For the suave sirocco of Sazerkind,
   And the pimpernell pellets of Pangipoo.

James C. Bayles.

BALLAD OF BEDLAM

OH, lady, wake! the azure moon
   Is rippling in the verdant skies,
   The owl is warbling his soft tune,
Awaiting but thy snowy eyes.
The joys of future years are past,
   To-morrow's hopes have fled away;
Still let us love, and e'en at last
   We shall be happy yesterday.

The early beam of rosy night
   Drives off the ebon morn afar,
While through the murmur of the light
   The huntsman winds his mad guitar.

Then, lady, wake! my brigantine
  Pants, neighs, and prances to be free;
Till the creation I am thine,
  To some rich desert fly with me.

Punch.

'T IS SWEET TO ROAM

'TIS sweet to roam when morning's light
    Resounds across the deep;
  And the crystal song of the woodbine bright
Hushes the rocks to sleep,
And the blood-red moon in the blaze of noon
  Is bathed in a crumbling dew,
And the wolf rings out with a glittering shout,
  To-whit, to-whit, to-whoo!

Anonymous.

HYMN TO THE SUNRISE

THE dreamy crags with raucous voices croon
    Across the zephyr's heliotrope career;
  I sit contentedly upon the moon
And watch the sunlight trickle round the sphere.

The shiny trill of jagged, feathered rocks
  I hear with glee as swift I fly away;
And over waves of subtle, woolly flocks
  Crashes the breaking day!

Anonymous.

THE MOON IS UP

THE moon is up, the moon is up!
  The larks begin to fly,
  And, like a drowsy buttercup,
Dark Phœbus skims the sky,
The elephant, with cheerful voice,
  Sings blithely on the spray;
The bats and beetles all rejoice,
  Then let me, too, be gay.

I would I were a porcupine,
  And wore a peacock's tail;
To-morrow, if the moon but shine,
  Perchance I'll be a whale.
Then let me, like the cauliflower,
  Be merry while I may,
And, ere there comes a sunny hour
  To cloud my heart, be gay!

Anonymous.

'T IS MIDNIGHT

'TIS midnight, and the setting sun
    Is slowly rising in the west;
    The rapid rivers slowly run,
The frog is on his downy nest.
The pensive goat and sportive cow,
Hilarious, leap from bough to bough.

Anonymous.

UPRISING SEE THE FITFUL LARK

UPRISING see the fitful lark
    Unfold his pinion to the stream;
    The pensive watch-dog's mellow bark
O'ershades yon cottage like a dream:
The playful duck and warbling bee
Hop gayly on, from tree to tree!

How calmly could my spirit rest
    Beneath yon primrose bell so blue,
And watch those airy oxen drest
    In every tint of pearling hue!
As on they hurl the gladsome plough,
While fairy zephyrs deck each brow!

Anonymous.

LIKE TO THE THUNDERING TONE

LIKE to the thundering tone of unspoke speeches,
    Or like a lobster clad in logic breeches,
Or like the gray fur of a crimson cat,
Or like the mooncalf in a slipshod hat;
E'en such is he who never was begotten
Until his children were both dead and rotten.

Like to the fiery tombstone of a cabbage,
Or like a crab-louse with its bag and baggage,
Or like the four square circle of a ring,
Or like to hey ding, ding-a, ding-a, ding;
E'en such is he who spake, and yet, no doubt,
Spake to small purpose, when his tongue was out.

Like to a fair, fresh, fading, wither'd rose,
Or like to rhyming verse that runs in prose,
Or like the stumbles of a tinder-box,
Or like a man that's sound yet sickness mocks;
E'en such is he who died and yet did laugh
To see these lines writ for his epitaph.

*Bishop Corbet
in 17th century.*

MY DREAM

I DREAMED a dream next Tuesday week,
    Beneath the apple-trees;
  I thought my eyes were big pork-pies,
And my nose was Stilton cheese.
The clock struck twenty minutes to six,
    When a frog sat on my knee;
I asked him to lend me eighteenpence,
    But he borrowed a shilling of me.

Anonymous.

MY HOME

MY home is on the rolling deep,
   I spend my time a-feeding sheep;
   And when the waves on high are running,
I take my gun and go a-gunning.
I shoot wild ducks down deep snake-holes,
And drink gin-sling from two-quart bowls.

Anonymous.

IN IMMEMORIAM

WE seek to know, and knowing seek;
   We seek, we know, and every sense
   Is trembling with the great intense,
And vibrating to what we speak.

We ask too much, we seek too oft;
   We know enough and should no more;
   And yet we skim through Fancy's lore,
And look to earth and not aloft.

  .   .   .   .

O Sea! whose ancient ripples lie
   On red-ribbed sands where seaweeds shone;
   O moon! whose golden sickle's gone,
O voices all! like you I die!

Cuthbert Bede.

THE HIGHER PANTHEISM IN A NUTSHELL

ONE, who is not, we see; but one, whom we see not, is;
Surely, this is not that; but that is assuredly this.

What, and wherefore, and whence: for under is over and under;
If thunder could be without lightning, lightning could be without thunder.

Doubt is faith in the main; but faith, on the whole, is doubt;
We cannot believe by proof; but could we believe without?

Why, and whither, and how? for barley and rye are not clover;
Neither are straight lines curves; yet over is under and over.

One and two are not one; but one and nothing is two;
Truth can hardly be false, if falsehood cannot be true.

Parallels all things are; yet many of these are askew;
You are certainly I; but certainly I am not you.

One, whom we see not, is; and one, who is not, we see;
Fiddle, we know, is diddle; and diddle, we take it, is dee.

A. C. Swinburne.

DARWINITY

POWER to thine elbow, thou newest of sciences,
    All the old landmarks are ripe for decay;
Wars are but shadows, and so are alliances,
    Darwin the great is the man of the day.

All other 'ologies want an apology;
    Bread's a mistake — Science offers a stone;
Nothing is true but Anthropobiology —
    Darwin the great understands it alone.

Mighty the great evolutionist teacher is,
    Licking Morphology clean into shape;
Lord! what an ape the Professor or Preacher is,
    Ever to doubt his descent from an ape.

A Nonsense Anthology

Man's an Anthropoid — he cannot help that, you know —
    First evoluted from Pongos of old;
He's but a branch of the *catarrhine* cat, you know —
    Monkey I mean — that's an ape with a cold.

Fast dying out are man's later Appearances,
    Cataclysmitic Geologies gone;
Now of Creation completed the clearance is,
    Darwin alone you must anchor upon.

Primitive Life — Organisms were chemical,
    Busting spontaneous under the sea;
Purely subaqueous, panaquademical,
    Was the original Crystal of Me.

I'm the Apostle of mighty Darwinity,
    Stands for Divinity — sounds much the same —
Apo-theistico-Pan-Asininity
    Only can doubt whence the lot of us came.

Down on your knees, Superstition and Flunkeydom!
    Won't you accept such plain doctrines instead?
What is so simple as primitive Monkeydom
    Born in the sea with a cold in its head?

Herman Merivale.

SONG OF THE SCREW

A MOVING form or rigid mass,
    Under whate'er conditions
Along successive screws must pass
    Between each two positions.
It turns around and slides along —
This is the burden of my song.

The pitch of screw, if multiplied
    By angle of rotation,
Will give the distance it must glide
    In motion of translation.
Infinite pitch means pure translation,
And zero pitch means pure rotation.

Two motions on two given screws,
    With amplitudes at pleasure,
Into a third screw-motion fuse;
    Whose amplitude we measure
By parallelogram construction
(A very obvious deduction.)

Its axis cuts the nodal line
    Which to both screws is normal,
And generates a form divine,
    Whose name, in language formal,
Is "surface-ruled of third degree."
Cylindroid is the name for me.

Rotation round a given line
> Is like a force along.
If to say couple you incline,
> You 're clearly in the wrong; —
'T is obvious, upon reflection,
A line is not a mere direction.

So couples with translations too
> In all respects agree;
And thus there centres in the screw
> A wondrous harmony
Of Kinematics and of Statics, —
The sweetest thing in mathematics.

The forces on one given screw,
> With motion on a second,
In general some work will do,
> Whose magnitude is reckoned
By angle, force, and what we call
The coefficient virtual.

Rotation now to force convert,
> And force into rotation;
Unchanged the work, we can assert,
> In spite of transformation.
And if two screws no work can claim,
Reciprocal will be their name.

Five numbers will a screw define,
> A screwing motion, six;
For four will give the axial line,
> One more the pitch will fix;

And hence we always can contrive
One screw reciprocal to five.

Screws — two, three, four or five, combined
    (No question here of six),
Yield other screws which are confined
    Within one screw complex.
Thus we obtain the clearest notion
Of freedom and constraint of motion.

In complex III., three several screws
    At every point you find,
Or if you one direction choose,
    One screw is to your mind;
And complexes of order III.
Their own reciprocals may be.

In IV., wherever you arrive,
    You find of screws a cone,
On every line in complex V.
    There is precisely one;
At each point of this complex rich,
A plane of screws have given pitch.

But time would fail me to discourse
    Of Order and Degree;
Of Impulse, Energy and Force,
    And Reciprocity.
All these and more, for motions small,
Have been discussed by Dr. Ball.

Anonymous.

MOORLANDS OF THE NOT

ACROSS the moorlands of the Not
    We chase the gruesome When;
And hunt the Itness of the What
Through forests of the Then.
Into the Inner Consciousness
    We track the crafty Where;
We spear the Ego tough, and beard
    The Selfhood in his lair.

With lassos of the brain we catch
    The Isness of the Was;
And in the copses of the Whence
    We hear the think bees buzz.
We climb the slippery Whichbark tree
    To watch the Thusness roll;
And pause betimes in gnostic rimes
    To woo the Over Soul.

Anonymous.

METAPHYSICS*

WHY and Wherefore set out one day
    To hunt for a wild Negation.
They agreed to meet at a cool retreat
On the Point of Interrogation.

* By permission of the author; from "The Bashful Earthquake," copyright, 1898.

But the night was dark and they missed their mark,
    And, driven well-nigh to distraction,
They lost their ways in a murky maze
    Of utter abstruse abstraction.

Then they took a boat and were soon afloat
    On a sea of Speculation,
But the sea grew rough, and their boat, though tough,
    Was split into an Equation.

As they floundered about in the waves of doubt
    Rose a fearful Hypothesis,
Who gibbered with glee as they sank in the sea,
    And the last they saw was this:

On a rock-bound reef of Unbelief
    There sat the wild Negation;
Then they sank once more and were washed ashore
    At the Point of Interrogation.

Oliver Herford.

ABSTROSOPHY *

IF echoes from the fitful past
    Could rise to mental view,
Would all their fancied radiance last
Or would some odors from the blast,
    Untouched by Time, accrue?

* By permission of the author; from "The Burgess Nonsense Book," copyright, 1901.

Is present pain a future bliss,
  Or is it something worse?
For instance, take a case like this:
Is fancied kick a real kiss,
  Or rather the reverse?

Is plenitude of passion palled
  By poverty of scorn?
Does Fiction mend where Fact has mauled?
Has Death its wisest victims called
  When idiots are born?

Gelett Burgess.

ABSTEMIA*

In Mystic Argot often Confounded with Farrago

IF aught that stumbles in my speech
    Or stutters in my pen,
  Or, claiming tribute, each to each,
  Rise, not to fall again,
Let something lowlier far, for me,
  Through evanescent shades —
Than which my spirit might not be
  Nourished in fitful ecstasy
Not less to know but more to see
  Where that great Bliss pervades.

Gelett Burgess

* By permission of the author; from "The Burgess Nonsense Book," copyright, 1901.

PSYCHOLOPHON *

Supposed to be Translated from the Old Parsee

TWINE then the rays
    Round her soft Theban tissues!
  All will be as She says,
When that dead past reissues.
Matters not what nor where,
  Hark, to the moon's dim cluster!
How was her heavy hair
  Lithe as a feather duster!
Matters not when nor whence;
  Flittertigibbet!
Sounds make the song, not sense,
    Thus I inhibit!

Gelett Burgess.

TIMON OF ARCHIMEDES †

AS one who cleaves the circumambient air
    Seeking in azure what it lacks in space,
    And sees a young and finely chiselled face
Filled with foretastes of wisdom yet more rare;
Touching and yet untouched — unmeasured grace!
  A breathing credo and a living prayer —
  Yet of the earth, still earthy; debonair
The while in heaven it seeketh for a place.

---

* By permission of the author; from "The Burgess Nonsense Book," copyright, 1901.

† By permission of R. H. Russell; from "Just Rhymes," copyright, 1899.

So thy dear eyes and thy kind lips but say —
  Ere from his cerements Timon seems to flit:
    "What of the reaper grim with sickle keen?"
And then the sunlight ushers in new day
  And for our tasks our bodies seem more fit —
    "Might of the night, unfleeing, sight unseen."

Charles Battell Loomis.

ALONE

ALONE! Alone!
  I sit in the solitudes of the moonshades,
    Soul-hungering in the moonshade solitudes sit I —
My heart-lifts beaten down in the wild wind-path.
Oppressed, and scourged and beaten down are my heart-lifts.
I fix my gaze on the eye-star, and the eye-star flings its dart upon me.
I wonder why my soul is lost in wonder why I am,
And why the eye-star mocks me,
Why the wild wind beats down my heart-lifts;
Why I am stricken here in the moonshade solitudes.
Oh! why am I what I am,
And why am I anything?
Am I not as wild as the wind and more crazy?
Why do I sit in the moonshade, while the eye-star mocks me while I ask what I am?
Why? Why?

Anonymous

A Nonsense Anthology

LINES BY A MEDIUM

I MIGHT not, if I could;
    I should not, if I might;
  Yet if I should I would,
    And, shoulding, I should quite!

I must not, yet I may;
    I can, and still I must;
  But ah! I cannot — nay,
    To must I may not, just!

I shall, although I will,
    But be it understood,
  If I may, can, shall — still
    I might, could, would, or should!

Anonymous.

TRANSCENDENTALISM

IT is told, in Buddhi-theosophic schools,
    There are rules,
By observing which, when mundane labor irks
One can simulate quiescence
By a timely evanescence
From his Active Mortal Essence,
    (Or his Works.)

The particular procedure leaves research
     In the lurch,
But, apparently, this matter-moulded form
     Is a kind of outer plaster,
     Which a well-instructed Master
     Can remove without disaster
          When he's warm.

And to such as mourn an Indian Solar Clime
          At its prime
'T were a thesis most immeasurably fit,
     So expansively elastic,
     And so plausibly fantastic,
     That one gets enthusiastic
          For a bit.

From the Times of India.

INDIFFERENCE

IN loopy links the canker crawls,
     Tads twiddle in their 'polian glee,
   Yet sinks my heart as water falls.
The loon that laughs, the babe that bawls,
The wedding wear, the funeral palls,
     Are neither here nor there to me.
       Of life the mingled wine and brine
     I sit and sip pipslipsily.

Anonymous.

[42]

QUATRAIN

OH! to be wafted away
    From this black Aceldama of sorrow,
   Where the dust of an earthy to-day
Makes the earth of a dusty to-morrow.

Anonymous.

COSSIMBAZAR

COME fleetly, come fleetly, my hookabadar,
    For the sound of the tam-tam is heard from afar.
"Banoolah! Banoolah!" The Brahmins are nigh,
And the depths of the jungle re-echo their cry.
    Pestonjee Bomanjee!
      Smite the guitar;
Join in the chorus, my hookabadar.

Heed not the blast of the deadly monsoon,
Nor the blue Brahmaputra that gleams in the moon.
Stick to thy music, and oh, let the sound
Be heard with distinctness a mile or two round.
    Jamsetjee, Jeejeebhoy!
      Sweep the guitar.
Join in the chorus, my hookabadar.

Art thou a Buddhist, or dost thou indeed
Put faith in the monstrous Mohammedan creed?
Art thou a Ghebir — a blinded Parsee?
Not that it matters an atom to me.
  Cursetjee Bomanjee!
  Twang the guitar
Join in the chorus, my hookabadar.

Henry S. Leigh.

THE PERSONIFIED SENTIMENTAL*

AFFECTION'S charm no longer gilds
 The idol of the shrine;
But cold Oblivion seeks to fill
 Regret's ambrosial wine.
Though Friendship's offering buried lies
 'Neath cold Aversion's snow,
Regard and Faith will ever bloom
 Perpetually below.

I see thee whirl in marble halls,
 In Pleasure's giddy train;
Remorse is never on that brow,
 Nor Sorrow's mark of pain.
Deceit has marked thee for her own;
 Inconstancy the same;
And Ruin wildly sheds its gleam
 Athwart thy path of shame.

Bret Harte.

* By permission of Houghton, Mifflin & Co., authorized publishers of Bret Harte's works.

A CLASSIC ODE *

OH, limpid stream of Tyrus, now I hear
    The pulsing wings of Armageddon's host,
  Clear as a colcothar and yet more clear —
(Twin orbs, like those of which the Parsees boast;)

Down in thy pebbled deeps in early spring
  The dimpled naiads sport, as in the time
When Ocidelus with untiring wing
  Drave teams of prancing tigers, 'mid the chime

Of all the bells of Phicol. Scarcely one
  Peristome veils its beauties now, but then —
Like nascent diamonds, sparkling in the sun,
  Or sainfoin, circinate, or moss in marshy fen.

Loud as the blasts of Tubal, loud and strong,
  Sweet as the songs of Sappho, aye more sweet;
Long as the spear of Arnon, twice as long,
  What time he hurled it at King Pharaoh's feet.

Charles Battell Loomis.

WHERE AVALANCHES WAIL

WHERE avalanches wail, and green Distress
    Sweeps o'er the pallid beak of loveliness:
    Where melancholy Sulphur holds her sway:
And cliffs of conscience tremble and obey;

* By permission of R. H. Russell; from "Just Rhymes," copyright, 1899.

And where Tartarean rattlesnakes expire;
Twisting like tendrils of a hero's pyre?
No! dancing in the meteor's hall of power,
See, Genius ponders o'er Affection's tower!
A form of thund'ring import soars on high,
Hark! 't is the gore of infant melody:
No more shall verdant Innocence amuse
The lips that death-fraught Indignation glues; —
Tempests shall teach the trackless tide of thought,
That undiminish'd senselessness is naught;
Freedom shall glare; and oh! ye links divine,
The Poet's heart shall quiver in the brine.

Anonymous.

BLUE MOONSHINE

MINGLED aye with fragrant yearnings,
    Throbbing in the mellow glow,
  Glint the silvery spirit-burnings,
Pearly blandishments of woe.

Aye! forever and forever,
  Whilst the love-lorn censers sweep,
Whilst the jasper winds dissever
  Amber-like the crystal deep,

Shall the soul's delirious slumber,
  Sea-green vengeance of a kiss,
Teach despairing crags to number
  Blue infinities of bliss.

Francis G. Stokes.

NONSENSE

Good reader, if you e'er have seen,
  When Phœbus hastens to his pillow,
  The mermaids with their tresses green
Dancing upon the western billow;
  If you have seen at twilight dim,
  When the lone spirit's vesper hymn
Floats wild along the winding shore,
The fairy train their ringlets weave
  Glancing along the spangled green; —
  If you have seen all this, and more,
God bless me! what a deal you 've seen!

Thomas Moore.

SUPERIOR NONSENSE VERSES

He comes with herald clouds of dust;
  Ecstatic frenzies rend his breast;
  A moment, and he graced the earth —
Now, seek him at the eagle's nest.

Hark! see'st thou not the torrent's flash
  Far shooting o'er the mountain height?
Hear'st not the billow's solemn roar,
  That echoes through the vaults of night?

Anon the murky cloud is riven,
  The lightnings leap in sportive play,
And through the clanging doors of heaven,
  In calm effulgence bursts the day.

Hope, peering from her fleecy car,
  Smiles welcome to the coming spring,
And birds with blithesome songs of praise
  Make every grove and valley ring.

What though on pinions of the blast
  The sea-gulls sweep with leaden flight?
What though the watery caverns deep
  Gleam ghostly on the wandering sight?

Is there no music in the trees
  To charm thee with its frolic mirth?
Must Care's wan phantom still beguile
  And chain thee to the stubborn earth?

Lo! Fancy from her magic realm
  Pours Boreal gleams adown the pole.
The tidal currents lift and swell —
  Dead currents of the ocean's soul.

Yet never may their mystic streams
  Breathe whispers of the mournful past,
Or Pallas wake her sounding lyre
  Mid Ether's columned temples vast.

Grave History walks again the earth
  As erst it did in days of eld,
When seated on the golden throne
  Her hand a jewelled sceptre held.

The Delphian oracle is dumb,
  Dread Cumae wafts no words of fate,
To fright the eager souls that press
  Through sullen Lethe's iron gate.

But deeper shadows gather o'er
    The vales that sever night and morn;
And darkness folds with brooding wing
    The rustling fields of waving corn.

Then issuing from his bosky lair
    The crafty tiger crouches low,
Or thunders from the frozen north
    The white bear lapped in Arctic snow.

Thus shift the scenes till high aloft
    The young moon sets her crescent horn,
And in gray evening's emerald sea
    The beauteous Star of Love is born.

Anonymous.

WHEN MOONLIKE ORE THE HAZURE SEAS

WHEN moonlike ore the hazure seas
    In soft effulgence swells,
    When silver jews and balmy breaze
Bend down the Lily's bells;
When calm and deap, the rosy sleap
    Has lapt your soal in dreems,
R Hangeline! R lady mine!
    Dost thou remember Jeames?

I mark thee in the Marble all,
    Where England's loveliest shine —
I say the fairest of them hall
    Is Lady Hangeline.

My soul, in desolate eclipse,
    With recollection teems —
And then I hask, with weeping lips,
    Dost thou remember Jeames?

Away! I may not tell thee hall
    This soughring heart endures —
There is a lonely sperrit-call
    That Sorrow never cures;
There is a little, little Star,
    That still above me beams;
It is the Star of Hope — but ar!
    Dost thou remember Jeames?

W. M. Thackeray.

LINES BY A PERSON OF QUALITY

FLUTTERING spread thy purple pinions,
    Gentle Cupid, o'er my heart,
I a slave in thy dominions,
    Nature must give way to art.

Mild Arcadians, ever blooming,
    Nightly nodding o'er your flocks,
See my weary days consuming,
    All beneath yon flowery rocks.

Thus the Cyprian goddess weeping,
    Mourned Adonis, darling youth:
Him the boar, in silence creeping,
    Gored with unrelenting tooth.

Cynthia, tune harmonious numbers;
  Fair Discretion, tune the lyre;
Soothe my ever-waking slumbers;
  Bright Apollo, lend thy choir.

Gloomy Pluto, king of terrors,
  Armed in adamantine chains,
Lead me to the crystal mirrors,
  Watering soft Elysian plains.

Mournful Cypress, verdant willow,
  Gilding my Aurelia's brows,
Morpheus, hovering o'er my pillow,
  Hear me pay my dying vows.

Melancholy, smooth Mæander,
  Swiftly purling in a round,
On thy margin lovers wander
  With thy flowery chaplets crowned.

Thus when Philomela, drooping,
  Softly seeks her silent mate,
So the bird of Juno stooping;
  Melody resigns to fate.

Alexander Pope.

FRANGIPANNI

UNTWINE those ringlets! Ev'ry dainty clasp
  That shines like twisted sunlight in my eye
Is but the coiling of the jewelled asp
That smiles to see men die.

Oh, cobra-curlèd! Fierce-fanged fair one! Draw
  Night's curtain o'er the landscape of thy hair!
I yield! I kneel! I own, I bless thy law
  That dooms me to despair.

I mark the crimson ruby of thy lips,
  I feel the witching weirdness of thy breath!
I droop! I sink into my soul's eclipse, —
  I fall in love with death!

And yet, vouchsafe a moment! I would gaze
  Once more into those sweetly-murderous eyes,
Soft glimmering athwart the pearly haze
  That smites to dusk the skies.

Hast thou no pity? Must I darkly tread
  The unknown paths that lead me wide from thee?
Hast thou no garland for this aching head
  That soon so low must be?

No sound? No sigh? No smile? Is *all* forgot?
  Then spin my shroud out of that golden skein
Thou callst thy tresses! *I* shall stay thee not —
  My struggles were but vain!

But shall I see thee far beyond the sun,
  When the new dawn lights Empyrean scenes?
What matters now? I know the poem's done,
  And wonder what the dickens it all means!

Anonymous.

LINES BY A FOND LOVER

LOVELY maid, with rapture swelling,
    Should these pages meet thine eye,
    Clouds of absence soft dispelling; —
Vacant memory heaves a sigh.

As the rose, with fragrance weeping,
    Trembles to the tuneful wave,
So my heart shall twine unsleeping,
    Till it canopies the grave.

Though another's smile 's requited,
    Envious fate my doom should be;
Joy forever disunited,
    Think, ah! think, at times on me!

Oft, amid the spicy gloaming,
    Where the brakes their songs instil,
Fond affection silent roaming,
    Loves to linger by the rill —

There, when echo's voice consoling,
    Hears the nightingale complain,
Gentle sighs my lips controlling,
    Bind my soul in beauty's chain.

Oft in slumber's deep recesses,
    I thy mirror'd image see;
Fancy mocks the vain caresses
    I would lavish like a bee!

But how vain is glittering sadness!
Hark, I hear distraction's knell!
Torture gilds my heart with madness!
Now forever fare thee well!

Anonymous.

FORCING A WAY

HOW many strive to force a way
   Where none can go save those who pay,
   To verdant plains of soft delight
The homage of the silent night,
When countless stars from pole to pole
Around the earth unceasing roll
In roseate shadow's silvery hue,
Shine forth and gild the morning dew.

And must we really part for good,
But meet again here where we've stood?
No more delightful trysting-place,
We've watched sweet Nature's smiling face.
No more the landscape's lovely brow,
Exchange our mutual breathing vow.
Then should the twilight draw around
No loving interchange of sound.

Less for renown than innate love,
These to my wish must recreant prove;
Nor whilst an impulse here remain,
Can ever hope the soul to gain;

For memory scanning all the past,
Relaxes her firm bonds at last,
And gives to candor all the grace
The heart can in its temple trace.

Anonymous.

THY HEART

THY heart is like some icy lake,
    On whose cold brink I stand;
  Oh, buckle on my spirit's skate,
And lead, thou living saint, the way
  To where the ice is thin —
That it may break beneath my feet
  And let a lover in!

Anonymous.

A LOVE-SONG BY A LUNATIC

THERE's not a spider in the sky,
    There's not a glowworm in the sea,
    There's not a crab that soars on high,
But bids me dream, dear maid, of thee!

When watery Phœbus ploughs the main,
  When fiery Luna gilds the lea,
As flies run up the window-pane,
  So fly my thoughts, dear love, to thee!

Anonymous.

THE PARTERRE

I DON'T know any greatest treat
    As sit him in a gay parterre,
  And sniff one up the perfume sweet
Of every roses buttoning there.

It only want my charming miss
    Who make to blush the self red rose;
Oh! I have envy of to kiss
    The end's tip of her splendid nose.

Oh! I have envy of to be
    What grass 'neath her pantoffle push,
And too much happy seemeth me
    The margaret which her vestige crush.

But I will meet her nose at nose,
    And take occasion for her hairs,
And indicate her all my woes,
    That she in fine agree my prayers.

The Envoy

I don't know any greatest treat
    As sit him in a gay parterre,
With Madame who is too more sweet
    Than every roses buttoning there.

E. H. Palmer.

TO MOLLIDUSTA

WHEN gooseberries grow on the stem of a daisy,
    And plum-puddings roll on the tide to the shore,
And julep is made from the curls of a jazey,
    Oh, then, Mollidusta, I'll love thee no more.

When steamboats no more on the Thames shall be going,
    And a cast-iron bridge reach Vauxhall from the Nore,
And the Grand Junction waterworks cease to be flowing,
    Oh, then, Mollidusta, I'll love thee no more.

Planché.

JOHN JONES

At the Piano

I

LOVE me and leave me; what love bids retrieve me? can June's fist grasp May?
Leave me and love me; hopes eyed once above me like spring's sprouts, decay;
Fall as the snow falls, when summer leaves grow false — cards packed for storm's play!

II

Nay, say Decay's self be but last May's elf, wing shifted, eye sheathed —
Changeling in April's crib rocked, who lets 'scape rills locked fast since frost breathed —
Skin cast (think!) adder-like, now bloom bursts bladder-like, — bloom frost bequeathed?

III

Ah, how can fear sit and hear as love hears it grief's heart's cracked grate's screech?
Chance lets the gate sway that opens on hate's way and shews on shame's beach
Crouched like an imp sly change watch sweet love's shrimps lie, a toothful in each.

IV

Time feels his tooth slip on husks wet from Truth's lip, which drops them and grins —
Shells where no throb stirs of life left in lobsters since joy thrilled their fins —
Hues of the pawn's tail or comb that makes dawn stale, so red for our sins!

V

Leaves love last year smelt now feel dead love's tears melt — flies caught in time's mesh!
Salt are the dews in which new time breeds new sin, brews blood and stews flesh;
Next year may see dead more germs than this weeded and reared them afresh.

VI

Old times left perish, new time to cherish; life
    just shifts its tune;
As, when the day dies, half afraid, eyes the growth
    of the moon;
Love me and save me, take me or waive me;
    death takes one so soon!

A. C. Swinburne.

THE OWL AND THE PUSSY-CAT

THE Owl and the Pussy-Cat went to sea
    In a beautiful pea-green boat:
    They took some honey, and plenty of money
Wrapped up in a five-pound note.
The Owl looked up to the stars above,
    And sang to a small guitar,
"Oh, lovely Pussy, oh, Pussy, my love,
    What a beautiful Pussy you are,
            You are,
            You are!
    What a beautiful Pussy you are!"

Pussy said to the Owl, "You elegant fowl,
    How charmingly sweet you sing!
Oh, let us be married; too long we have tarried:
    But what shall we do for a ring?"

They sailed away for a year and a day,
  To the land where the bong-tree grows;
And there in the wood a Piggy-wig stood,
  With a ring at the end of his nose,
          His nose,
          His nose,
  With a ring at the end of his nose.

"Dear Pig, are you willing to sell for one shilling
  Your ring?" Said the Piggy, "I will."
So they took it away and were married next day
  By the Turkey who lives on the hill.
They dined on mince and slices of quince,
  Which they ate with a runcible spoon;
And hand in hand, on the edge of the sand,
  They danced by the light of the moon,
          The moon,
          The moon,
  They danced by the light of the moon.

Edward Lear.

A BALLADE OF THE NURSERIE

SHE hid herself in the *soirée* kettle
  Out of her Ma's way, wise, wee maid!
  Wan was her lip as the lily's petal,
Sad was the smile that over it played.

Why doth she warble not? Is she afraid
Of the hound that howls, or the moaning mole?
 Can it be on an errand she hath delayed?
Hush thee, hush thee, dear little soul!

The nightingale sings to the nodding nettle
 In the gloom o' the gloaming athwart the glade:
The zephyr sighs soft on Popòcatapètl,
 And Auster is taking it cool in the shade:
 Sing, hey, for a *gutta serenade*!
Not mine to stir up a storied pole,
 No noses snip with a bluggy blade —
Hush thee, hush thee, dear little soul!

Shall I bribe with a store of minted metal?
 With Everton toffee thee persuade?
That thou in a kettle thyself shouldst settle,
 When grandly and gaudily all arrayed!
 Thy flounces 'ill foul and fangles fade.
Come out, and Algernon Charles 'ill roll
 Thee safe and snug in Plutonian plaid —
Hush thee, hush thee, dear little soul!

Envoi

When nap is none and raiment frayed,
And winter crowns the puddered poll,
 A kettle sings ane soote ballade —
Hush thee, hush thee, dear little soul.

John Twig.

A BALLAD OF HIGH ENDEAVOR

AH Night! blind germ of days to be,
    Ah me! ah me!
    (Sweet Venus, mother!)
What wail of smitten strings hear we?
    (Ah me! ah me!
        Hey diddle dee!)

Ravished by clouds our Lady Moon,
    Ah me! ah me!
    (Sweet Venus, mother!)
Sinks swooning in a lady-swoon
    (Ah me! ah me!
        Dum diddle dee!)

What profits it to rise i' the dark?
    Ah me! ah me!
    (Sweet Venus, mother!)
If love but over-soar its mark
    (Ah me! ah me!
        Hey diddle dee!)

What boots to fall again forlorn?
    Ah me! ah me!
    (Sweet Venus, mother!)
Scorned by the grinning hound of scorn,
    (Ah me! ah me!
        Dum diddle dee!)

Art thou not greater who art less?
    Ah me! ah me!
    (Sweet Venus, mother!)
Low love fulfilled of low success?
    (Ah me! ah me!
        Hey diddle dee!)

Anonymous.

THE LUGUBRIOUS WHING-WHANG *

OUT on the margin of moonshine land,
    Tickle me, love, in these lonesome ribs,
    Out where the whing-whang loves to stand,
Writing his name with his tail on the sand,
And wiping it out with his oogerish hand;
    Tickle me, love, in these lonesome ribs.

Is it the gibber of gungs and keeks?
    Tickle me, love, in these lonesome ribs,
Or what *is* the sound the whing-whang seeks,
Crouching low by the winding creeks,
And holding his breath for weeks and weeks?
    Tickle me, love, in these lonesome ribs.

Aroint him the wraithest of wraithly things!
    Tickle me, love, in these lonesome ribs,
'T is a fair whing-whangess with phosphor rings,
And bridal jewels of fangs and stings,

* By permission of the author; from "Rhymes of Childhood," copyright, 1890, 1898.

And she sits and as sadly and softly sings
As the mildewed whir of her own dead wings;
　　Tickle me, dear; tickle me here;
　　Tickle me, love, in these lonesome ribs.

James Whitcomb Riley.

OH! WEARY MOTHER

THE lilies lie in my lady's bower,
　　(Oh! weary mother, drive the cows to roost;)
They faintly droop for a little hour;
My lady's head droops like a flower.

She took the porcelain in her hand,
　　(Oh! weary mother, drive the cows to roost;)
She poured; I drank at her command;
Drank deep, and now — you understand!
　　(Oh! weary mother, drive the cows to roost.)

Barry Pain.

SWISS AIR *

I'M a gay tra, la, la,
　　With my fal, lal, la, la,
　　And my bright —
And my light —
　　Tra, la, le.　　　　　[*Repeat.*]

* By permission of Houghton, Mifflin & Co., authorized publishers of Bret Harte's works.

> Then laugh, ha, ha, ha,
> And ring, ting, ling, ling,
> And sing, fal, la, la,
>   La, la, le.   [*Repeat.*]
>
> *Bret Harte.*

THE BULBUL*

> THE bulbul hummeth like a book
>   Upon the pooh-pooh tree,
> And now and then he takes a look
>   At you and me,
>   At me and you.
>   Kuchi!
>   Kuchoo!
>
> *Owen Seaman.*

BALLAD

With an Ancient Refrain

> O STOODENT A has gone and spent,
>   With a hey-lililu and a how-low-lan
>   All his money to a Cent,
> And the birk and the broom blooms bonny.
>
> His Creditors he could not pay,
> With a hey-lililu and a how-low-lan,
> And Prison proved a shock to A,
> And the birk and the broom blooms bonny.
>
> *Anonymous.*

* By permission of John Lane; from "The Battle of the Bays."

OH, MY GERALDINE

OH, my Geraldine,
    No flow'r was ever seen so toodle um.
  You are my lum ti toodle lay,
    Pretty, pretty queen,
Is rum ti Geraldine and something teen,
More sweet than tiddle lum in May.
    Like the star so bright
    That somethings all the night,
      My Geraldine!
You're fair as the rum ti lum ti sheen,
    Hark! there is what — ho!
    From something — um, you know,
      Dear, what I mean.
Oh! rum! tum!! tum!!! my Geraldine.

F. C. Burnand.

BUZ, QUOTH THE BLUE FLY

BUZ, quoth the blue fly,
    Hum, quoth the bee,
  Buz and hum they cry,
    And so do we:
In his ear, in his nose, thus, do you see?
He ate the dormouse, else it was he.

*Ben Jonson
in " The Masque of Oberon."*

A SONG ON KING WILLIAM III

AS I walked by myself,
   And talked to myself,
     Myself said unto me,
Look to thyself,
Take care of thyself,
   For nobody cares for thee.

I answered myself,
And said to myself,
   In the self-same repartee,
Look to thyself,
Or not look to thyself,
   The selfsame thing will be.

Anonymous.

THERE WAS A MONKEY

THERE was a monkey climbed up a tree,
   When he fell down, then down fell he.

There was a crow sat on a stone,
When he was gone, then there was none.

There was an old wife did eat an apple,
When she had eat two, she had eat a couple.

There was a horse going to the mill,
When he went on, he stood not still.

There was a butcher cut his thumb,
When it did bleed, then blood did come.

There was a lackey ran a race,
When he ran fast, he ran apace.

There was a cobbler clouting shoon,
When they were mended, they were done.

There was a chandler making candle,
When he them strip, he did them handle.

There was a navy went into Spain,
When it returned, it came again.

Anonymous, 1626.

THE GUINEA PIG

THERE was a little Guinea-pig,
   Who, being little, was not big;
   He always walked upon his feet,
And never fasted when he eat.

When from a place he ran away,
He never at that place did stay;
And while he ran, as I am told,
He ne'er stood still for young or old.

He often squeaked, and sometimes vi'lent,
And when he squeaked he ne'er was silent:
Though ne'er instructed by a cat,
He knew a mouse was not a rat.

One day, as I am certified,
He took a whim, and fairly died;
And as I'm told by men of sense,
He never has been living since!

Anonymous.

THREE CHILDREN

THREE children sliding on the ice
    Upon a summer's day,
  As it fell out they all fell in,
    The rest they ran away.

Now, had these children been at home,
    Or sliding on dry ground,
Ten thousand pounds to one penny
    They had not all been drowned.

You parents all that children have,
    And you too that have none,
If you would have them safe abroad
    Pray keep them safe at home.

London, 1662.

IF

IF all the land were apple-pie,
    And all the sea were ink;
    And all the trees were bread and cheese,
What should we do for drink?

Anonymous.

A RIDDLE

THE man in the wilderness asked of me
    How many strawberries grew in the sea.
    I answered him as I thought good,
As many as red herrings grow in the wood.

Anonymous.

THREE JOVIAL HUNTSMEN

THERE were three jovial huntsmen,
    As I have heard them say,
    And they would go a-hunting
All on a summer's day.

All the day they hunted,
    And nothing could they find
But a ship a-sailing,
    A-sailing with the wind.

One said it was a ship,
  The other said Nay;
The third said it was a house
  With the chimney blown away.

And all the night they hunted,
  And nothing could they find;
But the moon a-gliding,
  A-gliding with the wind.

One said it was the moon,
  The other said Nay;
The third said it was a cheese,
  And half o't cut away.

Anonymous.

THREE ACRES OF LAND

My father left me three acres of land,
  Sing ivy, sing ivy;
My father left me three acres of land,
Sing holly, go whistle, and ivy!

I ploughed it with a ram's horn,
  Sing ivy, sing ivy;
And sowed it all over with one peppercorn,
  Sing holly, go whistle, and ivy!

I harrowed it with a bramble bush,
  Sing ivy, sing ivy;
And reaped it with my little penknife,
  Sing holly, go whistle, and ivy!

I got the mice to carry it to the barn,
  Sing ivy, sing ivy;
And thrashed it with a goose's quill,
  Sing holly, go whistle, and ivy!

I got the cat to carry it to the mill,
  Sing ivy, sing ivy;
The miller he swore he would have her paw,
And the cat she swore she would scratch his face,
  Sing holly, go whistle, and ivy!

Anonymous.

MASTER AND MAN

MASTER I have, and I am his man,
    Gallop a dreary dun;
  Master I have, and I am his man,
And I'll get a wife as fast as I can;
With a heighly gaily gamberally,
    Higgledy piggledy, niggledy, niggledy,
    Gallop a dreary dun.

Anonymous.

HYDER IDDLE

HYDER iddle diddle dell,
　　A yard of pudding is not an ell;
　　Not forgetting tweedle-dye,
A tailor's goose will never fly.

Anonymous.

KING ARTHUR

WHEN good King Arthur ruled the land,
　　He was a goodly king:
　　He stole three pecks of barley meal,
To make a bag-pudding.

A bag-pudding the king did make,
　　And stuffed it well with plums;
And in it put great lumps of fat,
　　As big as my two thumbs.

The king and queen did eat thereof,
　　And noblemen beside;
And what they could not eat that night,
　　The queen next morning fried.

Anonymous.

IN THE DUMPS

WE're all in the dumps,
    For diamonds are trumps;
    The kittens are gone to St. Paul's!
The babies are bit,
The moon's in a fit,
And the houses are built without walls.

Anonymous.

TWEEDLE-DUM AND TWEEDLE-DEE

TWEEDLE-DUM and Tweedle-dee
    Resolved to have a battle,
    For Tweedle-dum said Tweedle-dee
Had spoiled his nice new rattle.
Just then flew by a monstrous crow,
    As big as a tar-barrel,
Which frightened both the heroes so
    They quite forgot their quarrel.

Anonymous.

MARTIN TO HIS MAN

MARTIN said to his man,
    Fie! man, fie!
    Oh, Martin said to his man,
    Who's the fool now?
Martin said to his man,

Fill thou the cup, and I the can;
Thou hast well drunken, man:
    Who's the fool now?

I see a sheep shearing corn,
    Fie! man, fie!
I see a sheep shearing corn,
    Who's the fool now?
I see a sheep shearing corn,
And a cuckoo blow his horn;
Thou hast well drunken, man:
    Who's the fool now?

I see a man in the moon,
    Fie! man, fie!
I see a man in the moon,
    Who's the fool now?
I see a man in the moon,
Clouting of St. Peter's shoon,
Thou hast well drunken, man:
    Who's the fool now?

I see a hare chase a hound,
    Fie! man, fie!
I see a hare chase a hound,
    Who's the fool now?
I see a hare chase a hound,
Twenty mile above the ground;
Thou hast well drunken, man:
    Who's the fool now?

I see a goose ring a hog,
    Fie! man, fie!
I see a goose ring a hog,
    Who's the fool now?
I see a goose ring a hog,
And a snail that bit a dog;
Thou hast well drunken, man:
    Who's the fool now?

I see a mouse catch the cat,
    Fie! man, fie!
I see a mouse catch the cat,
    Who's the fool now?
I see a mouse catch the cat,
And the cheese to eat the rat;
Thou hast well drunken, man:
    Who's the fool now?

From *Deuteromelia*
printed in the reign of James I.

THE YONGHY-BONGHY-BO

I

ON the Coast of Coromandel
    Where the early pumpkins blow,
    In the middle of the woods
Lived the Yonghy-Bonghy-Bo.
Two old chairs, and half a candle,
One old jug without a handle,—

These were all his worldly goods:
In the middle of the woods,
These were all the worldly goods
Of the Yonghy-Bonghy-Bo,
Of the Yonghy-Bonghy-Bo.

II

Once, among the Bong-trees walking
  Where the early pumpkins blow,
    To a little heap of stones
    Came the Yonghy-Bonghy-Bo.
There he heard a Lady talking,
To some milk-white Hens of Dorking, —
    "'T is the Lady Jingly Jones!
    On that little heap of stones
    Sits the Lady Jingly Jones!"
Said the Yonghy-Bonghy-Bo,
Said the Yonghy-Bonghy-Bo.

III

"Lady Jingly! Lady Jingly!
  Sitting where the pumpkins blow,
    Will you come and be my wife?"
    Said the Yonghy-Bonghy-Bo,
"I am tired of living singly, —
On this coast so wild and shingly, —
    I'm a-weary of my life;
    If you'll come and be my wife,
    Quite serene would be my life!"
Said the Yonghy-Bonghy-Bo,
Said the Yonghy-Bonghy-Bo.

IV

"On this Coast of Coromandel
  Shrimps and watercresses grow,
    Prawns are plentiful and cheap,"
  Said the Yonghy-Bonghy-Bo.
"You shall have my chairs and candle,
And my jug without a handle!
    Gaze upon the rolling deep
    (Fish is plentiful and cheap):
    As the sea, my love is deep!"
  Said the Yonghy-Bonghy-Bo,
  Said the Yonghy-Bonghy-Bo.

V

Lady Jingly answered sadly,
  And her tears began to flow, —
    "Your proposal comes too late,
  Mr. Yonghy-Bonghy-Bo!
I would be your wife most gladly!"
(Here she twirled her fingers madly,)
    "But in England I 've a mate!
    Yes! you 've asked me far too late,
    For in England I 've a mate,
  Mr. Yonghy-Bonghy-Bo!
  Mr. Yonghy-Bonghy-Bo!

VI

"Mr. Jones (his name is Handel, —
  Handel Jones, Esquire & Co.)
    Dorking fowls delights to send,
  Mr. Yonghy-Bonghy-Bo!

Keep, oh, keep your chairs and candle,
And your jug without a handle, —
    I can merely be your friend!
    Should my Jones more Dorkings send,
    I will give you three, my friend!
Mr. Yonghy-Bonghy-Bo!
Mr. Yonghy-Bonghy-Bo!

VII

"Though you've such a tiny body,
  And your head so large doth grow, —
    Though your hat may blow away,
  Mr. Yonghy-Bonghy-Bo!
Though you're such a Hoddy Doddy,
Yet I wish that I could modi-
    fy the words I needs must say!
    Will you please to go away?
    That is all I have to say,
Mr. Yonghy-Bonghy-Bo!
Mr. Yonghy-Bonghy-Bo!"

VIII

Down the slippery slopes of Myrtle,
  Where the early pumpkins blow,
    To the calm and silent sea
  Fled the Yonghy-Bonghy-Bo.
There, beyond the Bay of Gurtle,
Lay a large and lively Turtle.
    "You're the Cove," he said, "for me:
    On your back beyond the sea,
    Turtle, you shall carry me!"

Said the Yonghy-Bonghy-Bo,
Said the Yonghy-Bonghy-Bo.

IX

Through the silent roaring ocean
  Did the Turtle swiftly go;
    Holding fast upon his shell
    Rode the Yonghy-Bonghy-Bo.
With a sad primæval motion
Toward the sunset isles of Boshen
    Still the Turtle bore him well,
    Holding fast upon his shell.
    "Lady Jingly Jones, farewell!"
Sang the Yonghy-Bonghy-Bo,
Sang the Yonghy-Bonghy-Bo.

X

From the Coast of Coromandel
  Did that Lady never go,
    On that heap of stones she mourns
    For the Yonghy-Bonghy-Bo.
On that Coast of Coromandel,
In his jug without a handle
    Still she weeps, and daily moans;
    On the little heap of stones
    To her Dorking Hens she moans,
For the Yonghy-Bonghy-Bo,
For the Yonghy-Bonghy-Bo.

Edward Lear.

THE POBBLE WHO HAS NO TOES

THE Pobble who has no toes
　　Had once as many as we;
　When they said, "Some day you may lose
　　　them all,"
He replied, "Fish fiddle de-dee!"
And his Aunt Jobiska made him drink
Lavender water tinged with pink;
For she said, "The World in general knows
There's nothing so good for a Pobble's toes!"

The Pobble who has no toes
　　Swam across the Bristol Channel;
But before he set out he wrapped his nose
　　In a piece of scarlet flannel.
For his Aunt Jobiska said, "No harm
Can come to his toes if his nose is warm;
And it's perfectly known that a Pobble's toes
Are safe — provided he minds his nose."

The Pobble swam fast and well,
　　And when boats or ships came near him,
He tinkledy-binkledy-winkled a bell
　　So that all the world could hear him.
And all the Sailors and Admirals cried,
When they saw him nearing the farther side,
"He has gone to fish for his Aunt Jobiska's
Runcible Cat with crimson whiskers!"

But before he touched the shore —
    The shore of the Bristol Channel,
A sea-green Porpoise carried away
    His wrapper of scarlet flannel.
And when he came to observe his feet,
Formerly garnished with toes so neat,
His face at once became forlorn
On perceiving that all his toes were gone!

And nobody ever knew,
    From that dark day to the present,
Whoso had taken the Pobble's toes,
    In a manner so far from pleasant.
Whether the shrimps or crawfish gray,
Or crafty mermaids stole them away,
Nobody knew; and nobody knows
How the Pobble was robbed of his twice five toes!

The Pobble who has no toes
    Was placed in a friendly Bark,
And they rowed him back and carried him up
    To his Aunt Jobiska's Park.
And she made him a feast at his earnest wish,
Of eggs and buttercups fried with fish;
And she said, "It's a fact the whole world knows,
That Pobbles are happier without their toes."

Edward Lear.

THE JUMBLIES

I

THEY went to sea in a sieve, they did;
  In a sieve they went to sea:
  In spite of all their friends could say,
On a winter's morn, on a stormy day,
  In a sieve they went to sea.
And when the sieve turned round and round,
And every one cried, "You'll all be drowned!"
They called aloud, "Our sieve ain't big;
But we don't care a button, we don't care a fig:
  In a sieve we'll go to sea!"
    Far and few, far and few,
      Are the lands where the Jumblies live;
      Their heads are green and their hands are blue;
      And they went to sea in a sieve.

II

They sailed away in a sieve, they did,
  In a sieve they sailed so fast,
With only a beautiful pea-green veil
Tied with a ribbon by way of a sail,
  To a small tobacco-pipe mast.
And every one said who saw them go,
"Oh! won't they soon be upset, you know?
For the sky is dark and the voyage is long,
And, happen what may, it's extremely wrong
  In a sieve to sail so fast."

Far and few, far and few,
    Are the lands where the Jumblies live;
   Their heads are green and their hands are blue;
    And they went to sea in a sieve.

III

The water it soon came in, it did;
   The water it soon came in:
So, to keep them dry, they wrapped their feet
In a pinky paper all folded neat;
   And they fastened it down with a pin.
And they passed the night in a crockery-jar;
And each of them said, "How wise we are!
Though the sky be dark, and the voyage be long,
Yet we never can think we were rash or wrong,
   While round in our sieve we spin."
    Far and few, far and few,
      Are the lands where the Jumblies live;
     Their heads are green and their hands are blue;
      And they went to sea in a sieve.

IV

And all night long they sailed away;
   And when the sun went down,
They whistled and warbled a moony song
To the echoing sound of a coppery gong,
   In the shade of the mountains brown.
"O Timballoo! How happy we are
When we live in a sieve and a crockery-jar!

And all night long, in the moonlight pale,
We sail away with a pea-green sail
  In the shade of the mountains brown."
    Far and few, far and few,
      Are the lands where the Jumblies live;
      Their heads are green, and their hands are blue;
      And they went to sea in a sieve.

V

They sailed to the Western Sea, they did, —
  To a land all covered with trees;
And they bought an owl and a useful cart,
And a pound of rice, and a cranberry-tart,
  And a hive of silvery bees;
And they bought a pig, and some green jackdaws,
And a lovely monkey with lollipop paws,
And forty bottles of ring-bo-ree,
  And no end of Stilton cheese.
    Far and few, far and few,
      Are the lands where the Jumblies live;
      Their heads are green, and their hands are blue;
      And they went to sea in a sieve.

VI

And in twenty years they all came back, —
  In twenty years or more;
And every one said, "How tall they 've grown!
For they 've been to the Lakes, and the Torrible Zone,
  And the hills of the Chankly Bore."

And they drank their health, and gave them a feast
Of dumplings made of beautiful yeast;
And every one said, "If we only live,
We, too, will go to sea in a sieve,
  To the hills of the Chankly Bore."
    Far and few, far and few,
      Are the lands where the Jumblies live;
      Their heads are green, and their hands are
        blue;
      And they went to sea in a sieve.

Edward Lear.

INCIDENTS IN THE LIFE OF MY UNCLE ARLY

I

OH! my aged Uncle Arly,
  Sitting on a heap of barley
    Through the silent hours of night,
Close beside a leafy thicket;
On his nose there was a cricket,
In his hat a Railway-Ticket,
    (But his shoes were far too tight.)

II

Long ago, in youth, he squander'd
All his goods away, and wander'd
    To the Timskoop-hills afar.

There on golden sunsets glazing
Every evening found him gazing,
Singing, "Orb! you're quite amazing!
    How I wonder what you are!"

III

Like the ancient Medes and Persians,
Always by his own exertions
    He subsisted on those hills;
Whiles, by teaching children spelling,
Or at times by merely yelling,
Or at intervals by selling
    "Propter's Nicodemus Pills."

IV

Later, in his morning rambles,
He perceived the moving brambles
    Something square and white disclose: —
'T was a First-class Railway-Ticket;
But on stooping down to pick it
Off the ground, a pea-green cricket
    Settled on my uncle's nose.

V

Never, nevermore, oh! never
Did that cricket leave him ever, —
    Dawn or evening, day or night;
Clinging as a constant treasure,
Chirping with a cheerious measure,
Wholly to my uncle's pleasure,
    (Though his shoes were far too tight.)

VI

So for three and forty winters,
Till his shoes were worn to splinters
    All those hills he wander'd o'er, —
Sometimes silent, sometimes yelling;
Till he came to Borley-Melling,
Near his old ancestral dwelling,
    (But his shoes were far too tight.)

VII

On a little heap of barley
Died my aged Uncle Arly,
    And they buried him one night
Close beside the leafy thicket;
There, his hat and Railway-Ticket;
There, his ever faithful cricket;
    (But his shoes were far too tight.)

Edward Lear.

LINES TO A YOUNG LADY

"HOW pleasant to know Mr. Lear!"
    Who has written such volumes of stuff!
Some think him ill-tempered and queer,
But a few think him pleasant enough.

His mind is concrete and fastidious,
    His nose is remarkably big;
His visage is more or less hideous,
    His beard it resembles a wig.

He has ears, and two eyes, and ten fingers,
  Leastways if you reckon two thumbs;
Long ago he was one of the singers,
  But now he is one of the dumbs.

He sits in a beautiful parlour,
  With hundreds of books on the wall;
He drinks a great deal of Marsala,
  But never gets tipsy at all.

He has many friends, laymen and clerical,
  Old Foss is the name of his cat:
His body is perfectly spherical,
  He weareth a runcible hat.

When he walks in a waterproof white,
  The children run after him so!
Calling out, "He's come out in his night-
  Gown, that crazy old Englishman, oh!"

He weeps by the side of the ocean,
  He weeps on the top of the hill;
He purchases pancakes and lotion,
  And chocolate shrimps from the mill.

He reads but he cannot speak Spanish,
  He cannot abide ginger-beer:
Ere the days of his pilgrimage vanish,
  How pleasant to know Mr. Lear.

Edward Lear.

WAYS AND MEANS

I'LL tell thee everything I can;
    There's little to relate.
I saw an aged aged man,
    A-sitting on a gate.
"Who are you, aged man?" I said,
    "And how is it you live?"
His answer trickled through my head
    Like water through a sieve.

He said, "I look for butterflies
    That sleep among the wheat:
I make them into mutton-pies,
    And sell them in the street.
I sell them unto men," he said,
    "Who sail on stormy seas;
And that's the way I get my bread —
    A trifle, if you please."

But I was thinking of a plan
    To dye one's whiskers green,
And always use so large a fan
    That they could not be seen.
So, having no reply to give
    To what the old man said,
I cried, "Come, tell me how you live!"
    And thumped him on the head.

A Nonsense Anthology

His accents mild took up the tale;
  He said, "I go my ways
And when I find a mountain-rill
  I set it in a blaze;
And thence they make a stuff they call
  Rowland's Macassar Oil —
Yet twopence-halfpenny is all
  They give me for my toil."

But I was thinking of a way
  To feed oneself on batter,
And so go on from day to day
  Getting a little fatter.
I shook him well from side to side,
  Until his face was blue;
"Come, tell me how you live," I cried,
  "And what it is you do!"

He said, "I hunt for haddock's eyes
  Among the heather bright,
And work them into waistcoat-buttons
  In the silent night.
And these I do not sell for gold
  Or coin of silvery shine,
But for a copper halfpenny
  And that will purchase nine.

"I sometimes dig for buttered rolls,
  Or set limed twigs for crabs;
I sometimes search the grassy knolls
  For wheels of Hansom cabs.

And that's the way " (he gave a wink)
   " By which I get my wealth —
And very gladly will I drink
   Your Honor's noble health."

I heard him then, for I had just
   Completed my design
To keep the Menai Bridge from rust
   By boiling it in wine.
I thanked him much for telling me
   The way he got his wealth,
But chiefly for his wish that he
   Might drink my noble health.

And now if e'er by chance I put
   My fingers into glue,
Or madly squeeze a right-hand foot
   Into a left-hand shoe,
Or if I drop upon my toe
   A very heavy weight,
I weep, for it reminds me so
Of that old man I used to know —
Whose look was mild, whose speech was slow,
Whose hair was whiter than the snow,
Whose face was very like a crow,
With eyes, like cinders, all aglow,
Who seemed distracted with his woe,
Who rocked his body to and fro,
And muttered mumblingly, and low,
As if his mouth were full of dough,

Who snorted like a buffalo —
That summer evening, long ago,
  A-sitting on a gate.

                              Lewis Carroll.

THE WALRUS AND THE CARPENTER

THE sun was shining on the sea,
  Shining with all his might:
He did his very best to make
  The billows smooth and bright —
And this was odd, because it was
  The middle of the night.

The moon was shining sulkily,
  Because she thought the sun
Had got no business to be there
  After the day was done —
"It's very rude of him," she said,
  "To come and spoil the fun!"

The sea was wet as wet could be,
  The sands were dry as dry.
You could not see a cloud, because
  No cloud was in the sky:
No birds were flying overhead —
  There were no birds to fly.

The Walrus and the Carpenter
    Were walking close at hand;
They wept like anything to see
    Such quantities of sand:
"If this were only cleared away,"
    They said, "it would be grand!"

"If seven maids with seven mops
    Swept it for half a year,
Do you suppose," the Walrus said,
    "That they could get it clear?"
"I doubt it," said the Carpenter,
    And shed a bitter tear.

"O Oysters come and walk with us!"
    The Walrus did beseech.
"A pleasant walk, a pleasant talk,
    Along the briny beach:
We cannot do with more than four,
    To give a hand to each."

The eldest Oyster looked at him,
    But not a word he said:
The eldest Oyster winked his eye,
    And shook his heavy head —
Meaning to say he did not choose
    To leave the oyster-bed.

But four young Oysters hurried up,
    All eager for the treat:
Their coats were brushed, their faces washed,

Their shoes were clean and neat —
And this was odd, because, you know,
  They had n't any feet.

Four other Oysters followed them,
  And yet another four;
And thick and fast they came at last,
  And more, and more, and more —
All hopping through the frothy waves,
  And scrambling to the shore.

The Walrus and the Carpenter
  Walked on a mile or so,
And then they rested on a rock
  Conveniently low:
And all the little Oysters stood
  And waited in a row.

"The time has come," the Walrus said,
  "To talk of many things:
Of shoes — and ships — and sealing-wax —
  Of cabbages — and kings —
And why the sea is boiling hot —
  And whether pigs have wings."

"But wait a bit," the Oysters cried,
  "Before we have our chat;
For some of us are out of breath,
  And all of us are fat!"
"No hurry!" said the Carpenter.
  They thanked him much for that.

"A loaf of bread," the Walrus said,
    "Is what we chiefly need :
Pepper and vinegar besides
    Are very good indeed —
Now if you're ready, Oysters dear,
    We can begin to feed."

"But not on us!" the Oysters cried,
    Turning a little blue.
"After such kindness that would be
    A dismal thing to do!"
"The night is fine," the Walrus said,
    "Do you admire the view?"

"It was so kind of you to come!
    And you are very nice!"
The Carpenter said nothing but
    "Cut us another slice :
I wish you were not quite so deaf —
    I've had to ask you twice!"

"It seems a shame," the Walrus said,
    "To play them such a trick,
After we've brought them out so far,
    And made them trot so quick!"
The Carpenter said nothing but
    "The butter's spread too thick!"

"I weep for you," the Walrus said;
    "I deeply sympathize."
With sobs and tears he sorted out

> Those of the largest size,
> Holding his pocket-handkerchief
> Before his streaming eyes.
>
> "O Oysters," said the Carpenter,
> "You 've had a pleasant run!
> Shall we be trotting home again?"
> But answer came there none —
> And this was scarcely odd, because
> They 'd eaten every one.
>
> *Lewis Carroll.*

THE HUNTING OF THE SNARK

> WE have sailed many months, we have sailed many weeks,
> (Four weeks to the month you may mark),
> But never as yet ('t is your Captain who speaks)
> Have we caught the least glimpse of a Snark!
>
> "We have sailed many weeks, we have sailed many days,
> (Seven days to the week I allow),
> But a Snark, on the which we might lovingly gaze,
> We have never beheld until now!
>
> "Come, listen, my men, while I tell you again
> The five unmistakable marks
> By which you may know, wheresoever you go,
> The warranted genuine Snarks.

"Let us take them in order. The first is the taste,
  Which is meagre and hollow, but crisp:
Like a coat that is rather too tight in the waist,
  With a flavour of Will-o-the-wisp.

"Its habit of getting up late you'll agree
  That it carries too far, when I say
That it frequently breakfasts at five-o'clock tea,
  And dines on the following day.

"The third is its slowness in taking a jest.
  Should you happen to venture on one,
It will sigh like a thing that is greatly distressed;
  And it always looks grave at a pun.

"The fourth is its fondness for bathing-machines,
  Which it constantly carries about,
And believes that they add to the beauty of scenes —
  A sentiment open to doubt.

"The fifth is ambition. It next will be right
  To describe each particular batch;
Distinguishing those that have feathers, and bite,
  From those that have whiskers, and scratch.

"For, although common Snarks do no manner of harm,
  Yet I feel it my duty to say
Some are Boojums — " The Bellman broke off in alarm,
  For the Baker had fainted away.

They roused him with muffins — they roused him
    with ice —
  They roused him with mustard and cress —
They roused him with jam and judicious advice —
  They set him conundrums to guess.

When at length he sat up and was able to speak,
  His sad story he offered to tell;
And the Bellman cried, "Silence! Not even a
    shriek!"
  And excitedly tingled his bell.

"My father and mother were honest, though
    poor —"
  "Skip all that!" cried the Bellman in haste,
"If it once becomes dark, there's no chance of a
    Snark,
  We have hardly a minute to waste!"

"I skip forty years," said the Baker, in tears,
  "And proceed without further remark
To the day when you took me aboard of your ship
  To help you in hunting the Snark.

"You may seek it with thimbles — and seek it with
    care;
  You may hunt it with forks and hope;
You may threaten its life with a railway-share;
  You may charm it with smiles and soap —

"I said it in Hebrew — I said it in Dutch —
    I said it in German and Greek;
But I wholly forgot (and it vexes me much)
    That English is what you speak!"

"The thing can be done," said the Butcher, "I think
    The thing must be done, I am sure.
The thing shall be done! Bring me paper and ink,
    The best there is time to procure."

So engrossed was the Butcher, he heeded them not,
    As he wrote with a pen in each hand,
And explained all the while in a popular style
    Which the Beaver could well understand.

"Taking Three as the subject to reason about —
    A convenient number to state —
We add Seven and Ten and then multiply out
    By One Thousand diminished by Eight.

"The result we proceed to divide, as you see,
    By Nine Hundred and Ninety and Two;
Then subtract Seventeen, and the answer must be
    Exactly and perfectly true.

"As to temper, the Jubjub's a desperate bird,
    Since it lives in perpetual passion:
Its taste in costume is entirely absurd —
    It is ages ahead of the fashion.

"Its flavor when cooked is more exquisite far
   Than mutton or oysters or eggs:
(Some think it keeps best in an ivory jar,
   And some, in mahogany kegs:)

"You boil it in sawdust; you salt it in glue:
   You condense it with locusts and tape;
Still keeping one principal object in view —
   To preserve its symmetrical shape."

The Butcher would gladly have talked till next day,
   But he felt that the Lesson must end,
And he wept with delight in attempting to say
   He considered the Beaver his friend.

Lewis Carroll.

SYLVIE AND BRUNO

He thought he saw a Banker's clerk
      Descending from the 'bus;
   He looked again, and found it was
      A Hippopotamus.
"If this should stay to dine," he said,
   "There won't be much for us!"

He thought he saw an Albatross
   That fluttered round the lamp:
He looked again, and found it was
   A Penny-Postage-Stamp.
"You'd best be getting home," he said;
   "The nights are very damp!"

He thought he saw a Coach-and-Four
  That stood beside his bed:
He looked again, and found it was
  A Bear without a Head.
" Poor thing," he said, " poor silly thing!
  It's waiting to be fed!"

He thought he saw a Kangaroo
  That worked a coffee-mill:
He looked again, and found it was
  A Vegetable-Pill.
" Were I to swallow this," he said,
  " I should be very ill!"

He thought he saw a Rattlesnake
  That questioned him in Greek:
He looked again, and found it was
  The Middle of Next Week.
" The one thing I regret," he said,
  " Is that it cannot speak!"

Lewis Carroll.

GENTLE ALICE BROWN

IT was a robber's daughter, and her name was Alice Brown.
  Her father was the terror of a small Italian town;
Her mother was a foolish, weak, but amiable old thing;
But it is n't of her parents that I'm going for to sing.

A Nonsense Anthology

As Alice was a-sitting at her window-sill one day,
A beautiful young gentleman he chanced to pass that way;
She cast her eyes upon him, and he looked so good and true,
That she thought, "I could be happy with a gentleman like you!"

And every morning passed her house that cream of gentlemen,
She knew she might expect him at a quarter unto ten,
A sorter in the Custom-house, it was his daily road
(The Custom-house was fifteen minutes' walk from her abode.)

But Alice was a pious girl, who knew it was n't wise
To look at strange young sorters with expressive purple eyes;
So she sought the village priest to whom her family confessed,
The priest by whom their little sins were carefully assessed.

"Oh, holy father," Alice said, "'t would grieve you, would it not?
To discover that I was a most disreputable lot!
Of all unhappy sinners I'm the most unhappy one!"
The padre said, "Whatever have you been and gone and done?"

A Nonsense Anthology

"I have helped mamma to steal a little kiddy from its dad,
I've assisted dear papa in cutting up a little lad.
I've planned a little burglary and forged a little check,
And slain a little baby for the coral on its neck!"

The worthy pastor heaved a sigh, and dropped a silent tear —
And said, "You mustn't judge yourself too heavily, my dear —
It's wrong to murder babies, little corals for to fleece;
But sins like these one expiates at half-a-crown apiece.

"Girls will be girls — you're very young, and flighty in your mind;
Old heads upon young shoulders we must not expect to find:
We mustn't be too hard upon these little girlish tricks —
Let's see — five crimes at half-a-crown — exactly twelve-and-six."

"Oh, father," little Alice cried, "your kindness makes me weep,
You do these little things for me so singularly cheap —
Your thoughtful liberality I never can forget;
But O there is another crime I haven't mentioned yet!

"A pleasant-looking gentleman, with pretty purple eyes,
I've noticed at my window, as I've sat a-catching flies;
He passes by it every day as certain as can be —
I blush to say I've winked at him and he has winked at me!"

"For shame," said Father Paul, "my erring daughter! On my word
This is the most distressing news that I have ever heard.
Why, naughty girl, your excellent papa has pledged your hand
To a promising young robber, the lieutenant of his band!

"This dreadful piece of news will pain your worthy parents so!
They are the most remunerative customers I know;
For many many years they've kept starvation from my doors,
I never knew so criminal a family as yours!

"The common country folk in this insipid neighborhood
Have nothing to confess, they're so ridiculously good;
And if you marry any one respectable at all,
Why, you'll reform, and what will then become of Father Paul?"

The worthy priest, he up and drew his cowl upon his crown,
And started off in haste to tell the news to Robber Brown;
To tell him how his daughter, who now was for marriage fit,
Had winked upon a sorter, who reciprocated it.

Good Robber Brown, he muffled up his anger pretty well,
He said, "I have a notion, and that notion I will tell;
I will nab this gay young sorter, terrify him into fits,
And get my gentle wife to chop him into little bits.

"I've studied human nature, and I know a thing or two,
Though a girl may fondly love a living gent, as many do —
A feeling of disgust upon her senses there will fall
When she looks upon his body chopped particularly small."

He traced that gallant sorter to a still suburban square;
He watched his opportunity and seized him unaware;
He took a life-preserver and he hit him on the head,
And Mrs. Brown dissected him before she went to bed.

And pretty little Alice grew more settled in her mind,
She nevermore was guilty of a weakness of the kind,
Until at length good Robber Brown bestowed her pretty hand
On the promising young robber, the lieutenant of his band.

W. S. Gilbert.

THE STORY OF PRINCE AGIB

STRIKE the concertina's melancholy string!
  Blow the spirit-stirring harp like any thing!
    Let the piano's martial blast
    Rouse the Echoes of the Past,
For of Agib, Prince of Tartary, I sing!

Of Agib, who amid Tartaric scenes,
Wrote a lot of ballet-music in his teens:
    His gentle spirit rolls
    In the melody of souls —
Which is pretty, but I don't know what it means.

Of Agib, who could readily, at sight,
Strum a march upon the loud Theodolite:
    He would diligently play
    On the Zoetrope all day,
And blow the gay Pantechnicon all night.

One winter — I am shaky in my dates —
Came two starving minstrels to his gates,
      Oh, Allah be obeyed,
        How infernally they played!
I remember that they called themselves the "Oiiaits."

Oh! that day of sorrow, misery, and rage,
I shall carry to the Catacombs of Age,
      Photographically lined
        On the tablet of my mind,
When a yesterday has faded from its page!

Alas! Prince Agib went and asked them in!
Gave them beer, and eggs, and sweets, and scents, and tin.
      And when (as snobs would say)
        They "put it all away,"
He requested them to tune up and begin.

Though its icy horror chill you to the core,
I will tell you what I never told before,
      The consequences true
        Of that awful interview,
For I listened at the key-hole in the door!

They played him a sonata — let me see!
"*Medulla oblongata*" — key of G.
      Then they began to sing
        That extremely lovely thing,
"Scherzando! ma non troppo, ppp."

He gave them money, more than they could count,
Scent, from a most ingenious little fount,
    More beer, in little kegs,
    Many dozen hard-boiled eggs,
And goodies to a fabulous amount.

Now follows the dim horror of my tale,
And I'm growing gradually pale,
    For, even at this day,
    Though its sting has passed away,
When I venture to remember it, I quail!

The elder of the brothers gave a squeal,
All-overish it made me for to feel!
    "Oh Prince," he says, says he,
    "*If a Prince indeed you be*,
I've a mystery I'm going to reveal!

"Oh, listen, if you'd shun a horrid death,
To what the gent who's speaking to you, saith:
    No 'Oiiaits' in truth are we,
    As you fancy that we be,
For (ter-remble) I am Aleck — this is Beth!"

Said Agib, "Oh! accursed of your kind,
I have heard that you are men of evil mind!"
    Beth gave a dreadful shriek —
    But before he'd time to speak
I was mercilessly collared from behind.

In number ten or twelve or even more,
They fastened me, full length upon the floor.
    On my face extended flat
    I was walloped with a cat
For listening at the key-hole of the door.

Oh! the horror of that agonizing thrill!
(I can feel the place in frosty weather still).
    For a week from ten to four
    I was fastened to the floor,
While a mercenary wopped me with a will!

They branded me, and broke me on a wheel,
And they left me in an hospital to heal;
    And, upon my solemn word,
    I have never never heard
What those Tartars had determined to reveal.

But that day of sorrow, misery, and rage,
I shall carry to the Catacombs of Age,
    Photographically lined
    On the tablet of my mind,
When a yesterday has faded from its page!
                        W. S. Gilbert.

FERDINANDO AND ELVIRA, OR THE GENTLE PIEMAN

"LOVE you?" said I, then I sighed, and then
    I gazed upon her sweetly —
For I think I do this sort of thing particularly neatly —

"Tell me whither I may hie me, tell me, dear one, that I may know —
Is it up the highest Andes? down a horrible volcano?"

But she said, "It isn't polar bears, or hot volcanic grottoes,
Only find out who it is that writes those lovely cracker mottoes."

Seven weary years I wandered — Patagonia, China, Norway,
Till at last I sank exhausted, at a pastrycook his doorway.

And he chirped and sang and skipped about, and laughed with laughter hearty,
He was wonderfully active for so very stout a party.

And I said, "Oh, gentle pieman, why so very, very merry?
Is it purity of conscience, or your one-and-seven sherry?"

. . . .

"Then I polish all the silver which a supper-table lacquers;
Then I write the pretty mottoes which you find inside the crackers."

"Found at last!" I madly shouted. "Gentle
 pieman, you astound me!"
Then I waved the turtle soup enthusiastically
 round me.

And I shouted and I danced until he'd quite a
 crowd around him,
And I rushed away, exclaiming, "I have found
 him! I have found him!"

W. S. Gilbert.

GENERAL JOHN

THE bravest names for fire and flames,
 And all that mortal durst,
 Were General John and Private James,
Of the Sixty-seventy-first.

General John was a soldier tried,
 A chief of warlike dons;
A haughty stride and a withering pride
 Were Major-General John.

A sneer would play on his martial phiz,
 Superior birth to show;
"Pish!" was a favorite word of his,
 And he often said "Ho! ho!"

Full-Private James described might be,
 As a man of mournful mind;
No characteristic trait had he
 Of any distinctive kind.

From the ranks, one day, cried Private James,
  "Oh! Major-General John,
I've doubts of our respective names,
  My mournful mind upon.

"A glimmering thought occurs to me,
  (Its source I can't unearth),
But I've a kind of notion we
  Were cruelly changed at birth.

"I've a strange idea, each other's names
  That we have each got on.
Such things have been," said Private James.
  "They have!" sneered General John.

"My General John, I swear upon
  My oath I think it is so —"
"Pish!" proudly sneered his General John,
  And he also said "Ho! ho!"

"My General John! my General John!
  My General John!" quoth he,
"This aristocratical sneer upon
  Your face I blush to see.

"No truly great or generous cove
  Deserving of them names
Would sneer at a fixed idea that's drove
  In the mind of a Private James!"

Said General John, "Upon your claims
    No need your breath to waste;
If this is a joke, Full-Private James,
    It's a joke of doubtful taste.

"But being a man of doubtless worth,
    If you feel certain quite
That we were probably changed at birth,
    I'll venture to say you're right."

So General John as Private James
    Fell in, parade upon;
And Private James, by change of names,
    Was Major-General John.

W. S. Gilbert.

LITTLE BILLEE

THERE were three sailors of Bristol City
    Who took a boat and went to sea,
    But first with beef and captain's biscuits,
And pickled pork they loaded she.

There was gorging Jack, and guzzling Jimmy,
    And the youngest he was little Billee.
Now when they'd got as far as the Equator,
    They'd nothing left but one split pea.

A Nonsense Anthology

Says gorging Jack to guzzling Jimmy,
  "I am extremely hungaree."
To gorging Jack says guzzling Jimmy,
  "We've nothing left, us must eat we."

Says gorging Jack to guzzling Jimmy,
  "With one another we shouldn't agree!
There's little Bill, he's young and tender,
  We're old and tough, so let's eat he."

"O Billy! we're going to kill and eat you,
  So undo the button of your chemie."
When Bill received this information,
  He used his pocket-handkerchie.

"First let me say my catechism,
  Which my poor mother taught to me."
"Make haste! make haste!" says guzzling Jimmy,
  While Jack pulled out his snicker-snee.

Then Bill went up to the main-top-gallant-mast,
  And down he fell on his bended knee,
He scarce had come to the Twelfth Commandment,
  When up he jumps — "There's land I see!"

"Jerusalem and Madagascar,
  And North and South Amerikee,
There's the British flag a-riding at anchor,
  With Admiral Napier, K.C.B."

So when they got aboard of the Admiral's,
   He hanged fat Jack and flogged Jimmee,
But as for little Bill, he made him
   The captain of a Seventy-three.

W. M. Thackeray.

THE WRECK OF THE "JULIE PLANTE" *

ON wan dark night on Lac St. Pierre,
   De win' she blow, blow, blow,
   An' de crew of de wood scow "Julie Plante"
Got scar't an' run below —
For de win' she blow lak hurricane;
   Bimeby she blow some more,
An' de scow bus' up on Lac St. Pierre
   Wan arpent from de shore.

De captinne walk on de fronte deck,
   An' walk de hin' deck too —
He call de crew from up de hole,
   He call de cook also.
De cook she's name was Rosie,
   She come from Montreal,
Was chambre maid on lumber barge,
   On de Grande Lachine Canal.

* By permission of G. P. Putnam's Sons; from "The Habitant,' copyright, 1897.

De win' she blow from nor'-eas'-wes', —
  De sout' win' she blow too,
W'en Rosie cry, "Mon cher captinne,
  Mon cher, w'at I shall do?"
Den de captinne t'row de big ankerre,
  But still de scow she dreef,
De crew he can't pass on de shore,
  Becos he los' hees skeef.

De night was dark lak wan black cat,
  De wave run high an' fas',
W'en de captinne tak' de Rosie girl
  An' tie her to de mas'.
Den he also tak' de life preserve,
  An' jomp off on de lak',
An' say, "Good-by, ma Rosie dear,
  I go down for your sak'."

Nex' morning very early
  'Bout ha'f-pas' two — t'ree — four —
De captinne — scow — an' de poor Rosie
  Was corpses on de shore.
For de win' she blow lak' hurricane,
  Bimeby she blow some more,
An' de scow, bus' up on Lac St. Pierre,
  Wan arpent from de shore.

Moral

Now all good wood scow sailor man
  Tak' warning by dat storm
An' go an' marry some nice French girl
  An' live on wan beeg farm.

De win' can blow lak' hurricane
  An' s'pose she blow some more,
You can't get drown on Lac St. Pierre
  So long you stay on shore.

William H. Drummond.

THE SHIPWRECK

UPON the poop the captain stands,
    As starboard as may be;
   And pipes on deck the topsail hands
To reef the topsail-gallant strands
  Across the briny sea.

" Ho! splice the anchor under-weigh! "
  The captain loudly cried;
" Ho! lubbers brave, belay! belay!
For we must luff for Falmouth Bay
  Before to-morrow's tide."

The good ship was a racing yawl,
  A spare-rigged schooner sloop,
Athwart the bows the taffrails all
In grummets gay appeared to fall,
  To deck the mainsail poop.

But ere they made the Foreland Light,
  And Deal was left behind,
The wind it blew great gales that night,
And blew the doughty captain tight,
  Full three sheets in the wind.

And right across the tiller head
  The horse it ran apace,
Whereon a traveller hitched and sped
Along the jib and vanished
  To heave the trysail brace.

What ship could live in such a sea?
  What vessel bear the shock?
"Ho! starboard port your helm-a-lee!
Ho! reef the maintop-gallant-tree,
  With many a running block!"

And right upon the Scilly Isles
  The ship had run aground;
When lo! the stalwart Captain Giles
Mounts up upon the gaff and smiles,
  And slews the compass round.

"Saved! saved!" with joy the sailors cry,
  And scandalize the skiff;
As taut and hoisted high and dry
They see the ship unstoppered lie
  Upon the sea-girt cliff.

And since that day in Falmouth Bay,
  As herring-fishers trawl,
The younkers hear the boatswains say
How Captain Giles that awful day
  Preserved the sinking yawl.

E. H. Palmer.

A SAILOR'S YARN *

As narrated by the second mate to one of the marines.

THIS is the tale that was told to me,
  By a battered and shattered son of the sea:
  To me and my messmate, Silas Green,
When I was a guileless young marine.

" 'T was the good ship ' Gyacutus,'
All in the China seas;
With the wind a lee, and the capstan free,
To catch the summer breeze.

" 'T was Captain Porgie on the deck
To the mate in the mizzen hatch,
While the boatswain bold, in the for'ard hold,
Was winding his larboard watch.

" ' Oh, how does our good ship head to-night?
How heads our gallant craft?'
' Oh, she heads to the E. S. W. by N.
And the binnacle lies abaft.'

" ' Oh, what does the quadrant indicate?
And how does the sextant stand?'
' Oh, the sextant 's down to the freezing point
And the quadrant 's lost a hand.'

* By permission of Houghton, Mifflin & Co.; from " Ballads of Blue Water," copyright, 1895.

"'Oh, if the quadrant's lost a hand,
And the sextant falls so low,
It's our body and bones to Davy Jones
This night are bound to go.

"'Oh, fly aloft to the garboard-strake,
And reef the spanker boom,
Bend a stubbing sail on the martingale
To give her weather room.

"'Oh, boatswain, down in the for'ard hold
What water do you find?'
'Four foot and a half by the royal gaff
And rather more behind.'

"'Oh, sailors, collar your marline spikes
And each belaying pin;
Come, stir your stumps to spike the pumps,
Or more will be coming in.'

"'They stirred their stumps, they spiked the pumps
They spliced the mizzen brace;
Aloft and alow they worked, but, oh!
The water gained apace.

"They bored a hole below her line
To let the water out,
But more and more with awful roar
The water in did spout.

"Then up spoke the cook of our gallant ship —
And he was a lubber brave —
'I've several wives in various ports,
And my life I'd like to save.'

"Then up spoke the captain of marines,
Who dearly loved his prog:
'It's awful to die, and it's worse to be dry,
And I move we pipes to grog.'

"Oh, then 't was the gallant second-mate
As stopped them sailors' jaw,
'T was the second-mate whose hand had weight
In laying down the law.

"He took the anchor on his back,
And leapt into the main;
Through foam and spray he clove his way,
And sunk, and rose again.

"Through foam and spray a league away
The anchor stout he bore,
Till, safe at last, I made it fast,
And warped the ship ashore."

This is the tale that was told to me,
By that modest and truthful son of the sea.
And I envy the life of a second mate,
Though captains curse him and sailors hate;
For he ain't like some of the swabs I've seen,
As would go and lie to a poor marine.

J. J. Roche.

THE WALLOPING WINDOW-BLIND *

A CAPITAL ship for an ocean trip
　　Was the "Walloping Window-blind" —
　No gale that blew dismayed her crew
　　Or troubled the captain's mind.
The man at the wheel was taught to feel
　　Contempt for the wildest blow,
And it often appeared, when the weather had cleared,
　　That he'd been in his bunk below.

The boatswain's mate was very sedate,
　　Yet fond of amusement, too;
And he played hop-scotch with the starboard watch,
　　While the captain tickled the crew.
And the gunner we had was apparently mad,
　　For he sat on the after rail,
And fired salutes with the captain's boots,
　　In the teeth of the booming gale.

The captain sat in a commodore's hat
　　And dined in a royal way
On toasted pigs and pickles and figs
　　And gummery bread each day.
But the cook was Dutch and behaved as such:
　　For the food that he gave the crew
Was a number of tons of hot-cross buns
　　Chopped up with sugar and glue.

* By permission of the author; from "Davy and the Goblin," copyright, 1884, 1885, by the Century Co.; 1885, by Ticknor & Co.

And we all felt ill as mariners will,
  On a diet that's cheap and rude;
And we shivered and shook as we dipped the cook
  In a tub of his gluesome food.
Then nautical pride we laid aside,
  And we cast the vessel ashore
On the Gulliby Isles, where the Poohpooh smiles,
  And the Anagazanders roar.

Composed of sand was that favored land,
  And trimmed with cinnamon straws;
And pink and blue was the pleasing hue
  Of the Tickletoeteaser's claws.
And we sat on the edge of a sandy ledge
  And shot at the whistling bee;
And the Binnacle-bats wore water-proof hats
  As they danced in the sounding sea.

On rubagub bark, from dawn to dark,
  We fed, till we all had grown
Uncommonly shrunk, — when a Chinese junk
  Came by from the torriby zone.
She was stubby and square, but we did n't much care,
  And we cheerily put to sea;
And we left the crew of the junk to chew
  The bark of the rubagub tree.

Charles E. Carryl.

THE ROLLICKING MASTODON *

A ROLLICKING Mastodon lived in Spain,
    In the trunk of a Tranquil Tree.
His face was plain, but his jocular vein
    Was a burst of the wildest glee.
His voice was strong and his laugh so long
    That people came many a mile,
And offered to pay a guinea a day
    For the fractional part of a smile.

The Rollicking Mastodon's laugh was wide —
    Indeed, 'twas a matter of family pride;
And oh! so proud of his jocular vein
    Was the Rollicking Mastodon over in Spain.

The Rollicking Mastodon said one day,
    "I feel that I need some air,
For a little ozone's a tonic for bones,
    As well as a gloss for the hair."
So he skipped along and warbled a song
    In his own triumphulant way.
His smile was bright and his skip was light
    As he chirruped his roundelay.

The Rollicking Mastodon tripped along,
    And sang what Mastodons call a song;
But every note of it seemed to pain
    The Rollicking Mastodon over in Spain.

* By permission of Lothrop Publishing Company; from "Wide Awake," copyright.

A Little Peetookle came over the hill,
   Dressed up in a bollitant coat;
And he said, "You need some harroway seed,
   And a little advice for your throat."
The Mastodon smiled and said, "My child,
   There's a chance for your taste to grow.
If you polish your mind, you'll certainly find
   How little, how little you know."

   The Little Peetookle, his teeth he ground
      At the Mastodon's singular sense of sound;
   For he felt it a sort of a musical stain
      On the Rollicking Mastodon over in Spain.

Alas! and alas! has it come to this pass?"
   Said the Little Peetookle. "Dear me!
It certainly seems your horrible screams
   Intended for music must be!"
The Mastodon stopped, his ditty he dropped,
   And murmured, "Good morning, my dear!
I never will sing to a sensitive thing
   That shatters a song with a sneer!"

   The Rollicking Mastodon bade him "adieu."
      Of course 't was a sensible thing to do;
   For Little Peetookle is spared the strain
      Of the Rollicking Mastodon over in Spain.

Arthur Macy.

THE SILVER QUESTION *

THE Sun appeared so smug and bright,
   One day, that I made bold
To ask him what he did each night
   With all his surplus gold.

He flushed uncomfortably red,
   And would not meet my eye.
"I travel round the world," he said,
   "And travelling rates are high."

With frigid glance I pierced him through.
   He squirmed and changed his tune.
Said he: "I will be frank with you:
   I lend it to the Moon.

"Poor thing! You know she's growing old
   And has n't any folk.
She suffers terribly from cold,
   And half the time she's broke."

. . . .

That evening on the beach I lay
   Behind a lonely dune,
And as she rose above the bay
   I buttonholed the Moon.

"Tell me about that gold," said I.
   I saw her features fall.
"You see, it's useless to deny;
   The Sun has told me all."

* By permission of the author; from the "Century Magazine," copyright, 1901.

"Sir!" she exclaimed, "how *can* you try
    An honest Moon this way?
As for the gold, I put it by
    Against a rainy day."

I smiled and shook my head. "All right,
    If you *must* know," said she,
"I change it into silver bright
    Wherewith to tip the Sea.

"He is so faithful and so good,
    A most deserving case;
If he should leave, I fear it would
    Be hard to fill his place."

   .   .   .   .

When asked if they accepted tips,
    The waves became so rough;
I thought of those at sea in ships,
    And felt I'd said enough.

For if one virtue I have learned,
    'T is *tact;* so I forbore
To press the matter, though I burned
    To ask one question more.

I hate a scene, and do not wish
    To be mixed up in gales,
But, oh, I longed to ask the Fish
    Whence came their silver scales!

Oliver Herford.

THE SINGULAR SANGFROID OF BABY BUNTING *

BARTHOLOMEW Benjamin Bunting
  Had only three passions in life,
And one of the trio was hunting,
  The others his babe and his wife.
And always, so rigid his habits,
  He frolicked at home until two,
And then started hunting for rabbits,
  And hunted till fall of the dew.

Belinda Bellonia Bunting,
  Thus widowed for half of the day,
Her duty maternal confronting,
  With baby would patiently play.
When thus was her energy wasted,
  A patented food she'd dispense.
(She had bought it the day that they pasted
  The posters all over her fence.)

But Bonaparte Buckingham Bunting,
  The infant thus blindly adored,
Replied to her worship by grunting,
  Which showed he was brutally bored.
'T was little he cared for the troubles
  Of life. Like a crab on the sands,
From his sweet little mouth he blew bubbles,
  And threatened the air with his hands.

* By permission of Harper & Brothers; from "Mother Goose for Grown-ups," copyright, 1900.

Bartholomew Benjamin Bunting
   One night, as his wife let him in,
Produced as the fruit of his hunting
   A cottontail's velvety skin,
Which, seeing young Bonaparte wriggle,
   He gave him without a demur,
And the babe with an aqueous giggle
   He swallowed the whole of the fur!

Belinda Bellonia Bunting
   Behaved like a consummate loon:
Her offspring in frenzy confronting
   She screamed herself mottled maroon:
She felt of his vertebræ spinal,
   Expecting he'd surely succumb,
And gave him one vigorous, final,
   Hard prod in the pit of his tum.

But Bonaparte Buckingham Bunting,
   At first but a trifle perplexed,
By a change in his manner of grunting
   Soon showed he was horribly vexed.
He displayed not a sign of repentance
   But spoke, in a dignified tone,
The only consecutive sentence
   He uttered. 'Twas: "Lemme alone."

The Moral: The parent that uses
   Precaution his folly regrets:
An infant gets all that he chooses,
   An infant chews all that he gets.

And colics?   He constantly has 'em
  So long as his food is the best,
But he'll swallow with never a spasm
  What ostriches could n't digest.

Guy Wetmore Carryl.

FAITHLESS NELLY GRAY

BEN BATTLE was a soldier bold,
    And used to war's alarms :
  But a cannon-ball took off his legs,
So he laid down his arms!

Now, as they bore him off the field,
  Said he, "Let others shoot,
For here I leave my second leg,
  And the Forty-second Foot!"

The army surgeons made him limbs :
  Said he, "They 're only pegs ;
But there 's as wooden members quite,
  As represent my legs!"

Now Ben he loved a pretty maid,
  Her name was Nelly Gray;
So he went to pay her his devours
  When he 'd devoured his pay!

But when he called on Nelly Gray,
    She made him quite a scoff;
And when she saw his wooden legs,
    Began to take them off!

"O Nelly Gray! O Nelly Gray!
    Is this your love so warm?
The love that loves a scarlet coat,
    Should be more uniform!"

Said she, "I loved a soldier once,
    For he was blithe and brave;
But I will never have a man
    With both legs in the grave!

"Before you had those timber toes,
    Your love I did allow,
But then you know, you stand upon
    Another footing now!"

"O Nelly Gray! O Nelly Gray!
    For all your jeering speeches,
At duty's call I left my legs
    In Badajos's breaches!"

"Why, then," said she, "you've lost the feet
    Of legs in war's alarms,
And now you cannot wear your shoes
    Upon your feats of arms!"

"Oh, false and fickle Nelly Gray;
  I know why you refuse:
Though I've no feet — some other man
  Is standing in my shoes!

"I wish I ne'er had seen your face;
  But now a long farewell!
For you will be my death — alas!
  You will not be my Nell!"

Now, when he went from Nelly Gray,
  His heart so heavy got —
And life was such a burden grown,
  It made him take a knot!

So round his melancholy neck
  A rope he did entwine,
And, for his second time in life
  Enlisted in the Line!

One end he tied around a beam,
  And then removed his pegs,
And as his legs were off, — of course,
  He soon was off his legs!

And there he hung till he was dead
  As any nail in town, —
For though distress had cut him up,
  It could not cut him down!

A dozen men sat on his corpse,
  To find out why he died —
And they buried Ben in four cross-roads,
  With a stake in his inside!

Thomas Hood.

THE ELDERLY GENTLEMAN

BY the side of a murmuring stream an elderly gentleman sat.
On the top of his head was a wig, and a-top of his wig was his hat.

The wind it blew high and blew strong, as the elderly gentleman sat;
And bore from his head in a trice, and plunged in the river his hat.

The gentleman then took his cane which lay by his side as he sat;
And he dropped in the river his wig, in attempting to get out his hat.

His breast it grew cold with despair, and full in his eye madness sat;
So he flung in the river his cane to swim with his wig, and his hat.

Cool reflection at last came across while this elderly gentleman sat;
So he thought he would follow the stream and look for his cane, wig, and hat.

His head being thicker than common, o'er-balanced
    the rest of his fat;
And in plumped this son of a woman to follow his
    wig, cane, and hat.

George Canning.

MALUM OPUS

PROPE ripam fluvii solus
    A senex silently sat;
    Super capitum ecce his wig,
Et wig super, ecce his hat.

Blew Zephyrus alte, acerbus,
    Dum elderly gentleman sat;
Et a capite took up quite torve
    Et in rivum projecit his hat.

Tunc soft maledixit the old man,
    Tunc stooped from the bank where he sat
Et cum scipio poked in the water,
    Conatus servare his hat.

Blew Zephyrus alte, acerbus,
    The moment it saw him at that;
Et whisked his novum scratch wig
    In flumen, along with his hat.

Ab imo pectore damnavit
  In cœruleus eye dolor sat;
Tunc despairingly threw in his cane
  Nare cum his wig and his hat.

L'Envoi

Contra bonos mores, don't swear
  It 'est wicked you know (verbum sat),
Si this tale habet no other moral
  Mehercle! You 're gratus to that!

James Appleton Morgan.

ÆSTIVATION *

IN candent ire the solar splendor flames;
  The foles, languescent, pend from arid rames;
  His humid front the cive, anheling, wipes,
And dreams of erring on ventiferous ripes.

How dulce to vive occult to mortal eyes,
Dorm on the herb with none to supervise,
Carp the suave berries from the crescent vine,
And bibe the flow from longicaudate kine.

To me also, no verdurous visions come
Save you exiguous pool's confervascum, —
No concave vast repeats the tender hue
That laves my milk-jug with celestial blue.

* By permission of Houghton, Mifflin & Co., authorized publishers.

Me wretched ! Let me curr to quercine shades !
Effund your albid hausts, lactiferous maids !
Oh, might I vole to some umbrageous chump, —
Depart, — be off, — excede, — evade, — erump !

O. W. Holmes.

A HOLIDAY TASK

Air — Jullien's Polka

QUI nunc dancere vult modo
    Wants to dance in the fashion, oh !
    Discere debet — ought to know,
Kickere floor cum heel et toe
        One, two three,
        Hop with me,
Whirligig, twirligig, rapidè.

Polkam jungere, Virgo, vis,
Will you join the Polka, Miss ?
Liberius — most willingly.
Sic agimus — then let us try :
        Nunc vide
        Skip with me,
Whirlabout, roundabout, celerè.

Tum lævâ citò, tum dextrâ
First to the left, and then t' other way ;
Aspice retrò in vultu,
You look at her, and she looks at you.

Das palmam,
Change hands ma'am
Celerè — run away, just in sham.

Gilbert Abbott à Becket.

PUER EX JERSEY

PUER ex Jersey
   Iens ad school;
  Vidit in meadow,
Infestum mule.

Ille approaches
O magnus sorrow!
Puer it skyward.
Funus ad morrow.

Moral

Qui vidit a thing
Non ei well-known,
Est bene for him
Relinqui id alone.

Anonymous.

THE LITTLE PEACH

UNE petite pêche dans un orchard fleurit,
   Attendez à mon narration triste!
  Une petite pêche verdante fleurit.
Grâce à chaleur de soleil, et moisture de miste.
Il fleurit, il fleurit,
   Attendez à mon narration triste!

Signes dures pour les deux,
Petit Jean et sa sœur Sue,
Et la pêche d'une verdante hue,
Qui fleurit, qui fleurit,
Attendez à mon narration triste!

Anonymous.

MONSIEUR McGINTÉ

MONSIEUR McGinté allait en bas jusqu'au
    fond du mer,
  Ils ne l'ont pas encore trouvé
Je crois qu'il est certainement mouillé.
Monsieur McGinté, je le repéte, allait jusqu'au
    fond du mer,
  Habillé dans sa meilleure costume.

Anonymous.

YE LAYE OF YE WOODPECKORE

Picus Erythrocephalus:

O WHITHER goest thou, pale stúdent
    Within the wood so fur?
  Art on the chokesome cherry bent?
Dost seek the chestnut burr?

Pale Studént.

> O it is not for the mellow chestnút
>   That I so far am come,
> Nor yet for puckery cherries, but
>   For Cypripediúm.

> A blossom hangs the choke-cherry
>   And eke the chestnut burr,
> And thou a silly fowl must be,
>   Thou red-head wood-peckér.

Picus Erythrocephalus:

> Turn back, turn back, thou pale studént,
>   Nor in the forest go;
> There lurks beneath his bosky tent
>   The deadly mosquitó,

> And there the wooden-chuck doth tread,
>   And from the oak-tree's top
> The red, red squirrels on thy head
>   The frequent acorn drop.

Pale Studént.

> The wooden-chuck is next of kin
>   Unto the wood-peckér:
> I fear not thine ill-boding din,
>   And why should I fear her?

What though a score of acorns drop
    And squirrels' fur be red !
'T is not so ruddy as thy top —
    So scarlet as thy head.

O rarely blooms the Cypripe-
    diúm upon its stalk;
And like a torch it shines to me
    Adown the dark wood-walk.

O joy to pluck it from the ground,
    To view the purple sac,
To touch the sessile stigma's round —
    And shall I then turn back ?

Picus Erythrocephalus:

O black and shining is the log
    That feeds the sumptuous weed,
Nor stone is found nor bedded log
    Where foot may well proceed.

Midmost it glimmers in the mire
    Like Jack o' Lanthorn's spark,
Lighting, with phosphorescent fire,
    The green umbrageous dark.

There while thy thirsty glances drink
    The fair and baneful plant,
Thy shoon within the ooze shall sink
    And eke thine either pant.

Pale Studént.

> Give o'er, give o'er, thou wood-peckóre;
>   The bark upon the tree,
> Thou, at thy will, mayst peck and bore
>   But peck and bore not me.
>
> Full two long hours I've searched about
>   And 't would in sooth be rum,
> If I should now go back without
>   The Cypripediúm.

Picus Erythrocephalus:

> Farewell! Farewell! But this I tell
>   To thee, thou pale studént,
> Ere dews have fell, thou 'lt rue it well
>   That woodward thou didst went:
>
> Then whilst thou blows the drooping nose
>   And wip'st the pensive eye —
> There where the sad *symplocarpus fœtidus* grows,
>   Then think — O think of I!
>
> Loud flouted there that student wight
>   Solche warnynge for to hear;
> "I scorn, old hen, thy threats of might,
>   And eke thine ill grammére.
>
> "Go peck the lice (or green or red)
>   That swarm the bass-wood tree,
> But wag no more thine addled head
>   Nor clack thy tongue at me."

The wood-peck turned to whet her beak,
    The student heard her drum,
As through the wood he went to seek
    The Cypripediúm.

Alas! and for that pale studént:
    The evening bell did ring,
And down the walk the Freshmen went
    Unto the prayer-meetíng;

Upon the fence loud rose the song,
    The weak, weak tea was o'er —
Ha! who is he that sneaks along
    Into South Middle's door?

The mud was on his shoon, and O!
    The briar was in his thumb,
His staff was in his hand but no —
    No Cypripediúm.

Henry A. Beers.

COLLUSION BETWEEN A ALE-GAITER AND A WATER-SNAIK

THERE is a niland on a river lying,
    Which runs into Gautimaly, a warm country,
    Lying near the Tropicks, covered with sand;
Hear and their a symptom of a Wilow,
Hanging of its umberagious limbs & branches
Over the clear streme meandering far below.
This was the home of the now silent Alegaiter,

When not in his other element confine'd:
Here he wood set upon his eggs asleep
With 1 ey observant of flis and other passing
Objects: a while it kept a going on so:
Fereles of danger was the happy Alegaiter!
But a las! in a nevil our he was fourced to
Wake! that dreme of Blis was two sweet for him.
1 morning the sun arose with unusool splender
Whitch allso did our Alegaiter, coming from the water,
His scails a flinging of the rais of the son back,
To the fountain-head which tha originly sprung from,
But having not had nothing to eat for some time, he
Was slepy and gap'd, in a short time, widely.
Unfoalding soon a welth of perl-white teth,
The rais of the son soon shet his sinister ey
Because of their mutool splendor and warmth.
The evil Our (which I sed) was now come;
Evidently a good chans for a water-snaik
Of the large specie, which soon appeared
Into the horison, near the bank where reposed
Calmly in slepe the Alegaiter before spoken of.
About 60 feet was his Length (not the 'gaiter)
And he was aperiently a well-proportioned snaik.
When he was all ashore he glared upon
The iland with approval, but was soon
"Astonished with the view and lost to wonder"
(from Wats)
(For jest then he began to see the Alegaiter)
Being a nateral enemy of his'n, he worked hisself
Into a fury, also a ni position.

A Nonsense Anthology

Before the Alegaiter well could ope
His eye (in other words perceive his danger)
The Snaik had enveloped his body just 19
Times with " foalds voluminous and vast" (from
    Milton)
And had tore off several scails in the confusion,
Besides squeazing him awfully into his stomoc.
Just then, by a fortinate turn in his affairs,
He ceazed into his mouth the careless tale
Of the unreflecting water-snaik! Grown desperate
He, finding that his tale was fast squesed
Terrible while they roaled all over the iland.

It was a well-conduckted Affair; no noise
Disturbed the harmony of the seen, ecsept
Onct when a Willow was snaped into by the roaling.
Eeach of the combatence hadn't a minit for holering.
So the conflick was naterally tremenjous!
But soon by grate force the tail was bit complete-
Ly of; but the eggzeration was too much
For his delicate Constitootion; he felt a compres-
    sion
Onto his chest and generally over his body;
When he ecspressed his breathing, it was with
Grate difficulty that he felt inspired again onct more.
Of course this state must suffer a revolootion.
So the alegaiter give but one yel, and egspired.
The water-snaik realed hisself off, & survay'd
For say 10 minits, the condition of
His fo: then wondering what made his tail hurt,
He slowly went off for to cool.

                              J. W. Morris.

ODD TO A KROKIS

SELESTIAL apoley which Didest inspire.
  the souls of burns and pop with sackred fir.
  Kast thy Mantil over me When i shal sing.
the praiz Of A sweat flower who grows in spring.
Which has of late kome under the Fokis.
of My eyes. It is called a krokis.
Sweat lovly prety littil sweat Thing.
you bloometh before The lairicks on High sing.
thy lefs are neithir Red Nor yelly.
but Just betwixt the two you hardy felly.

i fear youl yet be Nippit with the frost.
As Maney a one has known to there kost.
you should have not kome out in such a hurrey.
As this is only the Month of Febrywurrey.
and you may expick yet Much bad wethir.
when all your blads will krunkil up like Burn
      leather.
alas. alas. theres Men which tries to rime.
who have like you kome out befor there time.
The Moril of My peese depend upon it.
is good so here i End my odd or sonit.

Anonymous

SOME VERSES TO SNAIX

PRODIGGUS reptile! long and skaly kuss!
   You are the dadrattedest biggest thing I ever
   Seed that cud ty itself into a double bo-
Not, and cum all strate again in a
Minnit or so, without winkin or seemin
To experience any particular pane
In the diafram.

Stoopenjus inseck! marvelous annimile!
You are no doubt seven thousand yeres
Old, and hav a considerable of a
Family sneekin round thru the tall
Gras in Africa, a eetin up little greezy
Piggers, and wishin they was biggir.

I wonder how big yu was when yu
Was a inphant about 2 fete long. I
Expec yu was a purty good size, and
Lived on phrogs, and lizzerds, and polly-
Wogs and sutch things.

You are havin' a nice time now, ennyhow —
Don't have nothing to do but lay oph.
And ete kats and rabbits, and stic
Out yure tung and twist yur tale.
I wunder if yu ever swollered a man
Without takin oph his butes. If there was
Brass buttins on his kote, I spose

[147]

Yu had ter swaller a lot of buttin-
Wholes, and a shu-hamer to nock
The soals oph of the boots and drive in
The tax, so that they would n't kut yure
Inside. I wunder if vittles taste
Good all the way down. I expec so —
At leest, fur 6 or 7 fete.

You are so mighty long, I shud thynk
If your tale was kold, yure hed
Woodent no it till the next day,
But it 's hard tu tell : snaix is snaix.

Anonymous.

A GREAT MAN

YE muses, pour the pitying tear
    For Pollio snatch'd away :
    For had he liv'd another year !
— He had not dy'd to-day.

O, were he born to bless mankind,
    In virtuous times of yore,
Heroes themselves had fallen behind !
    — Whene'er he went before.

How sad the groves and plains appear,
    And sympathetic sheep :
Even pitying hills would drop a tear !
    — If hills could learn to weep.

His bounty in exalted strain
   Each bard might well display:
Since none implor'd relief in vain!
   — That went reliev'd away.

And hark! I hear the tuneful throng;
   His obsequies forbid.
He still shall live, shall live as long
   — As ever dead man did.

Oliver Goldsmith.

AN ELEGY

On the Glory of her Sex, Mrs. Mary Blaize

GOOD people all, with one accord,
   Lament for Madam Blaize,
Who never wanted a good word —
   From those who spoke her praise.

The needy seldom pass'd her door,
   And always found her kind;
She freely lent to all the poor —
   Who left a pledge behind.

She strove the neighborhood to please
   With manners wondrous winning;
And never follow'd wicked ways —
   Unless when she was sinning.

At church, in silks and satins new,
  With hoop of monstrous size,
She never slumber'd in her pew —
  But when she shut her eyes.

Her love was sought, I do aver,
  By twenty beaux and more;
The King himself has follow'd her —
  When she has walk'd before.

But now, her wealth and finery fled,
  Her hangers-on cut short all;
The doctors found, when she was dead —
  Her last disorder mortal.

Let us lament, in sorrow sore,
  For Kent Street well may say,
That had she lived a twelvemonth more —
  She had not died to-day.
                              Oliver Goldsmith.

PARSON GRAY

A QUIET home had Parson Gray,
    Secluded in a vale;
  His daughters ail were feminine,
And all his sons were male.

How faithfully did Parson Gray
  The bread of life dispense —
Well "posted" in theology,
  And post and rail his fence.

'Gainst all the vices of the age
  He manfully did battle;
His chickens were a biped breed,
  And quadruped his cattle.

No clock more punctually went,
  He ne'er delayed a minute —
Nor ever empty was his purse,
  When he had money in it.

His piety was ne'er denied;
  His truths hit saint and sinner;
At morn he always breakfasted;
  He always dined at dinner.

He ne'er by any luck was grieved,
  By any care perplexed —
No filcher he, though when he preached,
  He always "took" a text.

As faithful characters he drew
  As mortal ever saw;
But ah! poor parson! when he died,
  His breath he could not draw!

Oliver Goldsmith.

AN ELEGY ON THE DEATH OF A MAD DOG

GOOD people all, of every sort,
  Give ear unto my song;
  And if you find it wondrous short, —
It cannot hold you long.

In Islington there was a man,
   Of whom the world might say
That still a godly race he ran, —
   Whene'er he went to pray.

A kind and gentle heart he had,
   To comfort friends and foes;
The naked every day he clad, —
   When he put on his clothes.

And in that town a dog was found,
   As many dogs there be,
Both mongrel, puppy, whelp, and hound,
   And curs of low degree.

The dog and man at first were friends;
   But when a pique began,
The dog, to gain some private ends,
   Went mad, and bit the man.

Around from all the neighboring streets,
   The wondering neighbors ran,
And swore the dog had lost his wits
   To bite so good a man.

The wound it seemed both sore and sad
   To every Christian eye;
And while they swore the dog was mad
   They swore the man would die.

But soon a wonder came to light,
   That showed the rogues they lied;
The man recovered of the bite,
   The dog it was that died.

Oliver Goldsmith.

THE WONDERFUL OLD MAN

THERE was an old man
   Who lived on a common
   And, if fame speaks true,
He was born of a woman.
Perhaps you will laugh,
   But for truth I 've been told
He once was an infant
   Tho' age made him old.

Whene'er he was hungry
   He longed for some meat;
And if he could get it
   'T was said he would eat.
When thirsty he 'd drink
   If you gave him a pot,
And what he drank mostly
   Ran down his throat.

He seldom or never
   Could see without light,
And yet I 've been told he
   Could hear in the night.

He has oft been awake
  In the daytime, 't is said,
And has fallen asleep
  As he lay in his bed.

'T is reported his tongue
  Always moved when he talk'd,
And he stirred both his arms
  And his legs when he walk'd;
And his gait was so odd
  Had you seen him you 'd burst,
For one leg or t' other
  Would always be first.

His face was the drollest
  That ever was seen,
For if 't was not washed
  It seldom was clean;
His teeth he expos'd when
  He happened to grin,
And his mouth stood across
  'Twixt his nose and his chin.

When this whimsical chap
  Had a river to pass,
If he could n't get over
  He stayed where he was.
'T is said he ne'er ventured
  To quit the dry ground,
Yet so great was his luck
  He never was drowned.

At last he fell sick,
  As old chronicles tell,
And then, as folks say,
  He was not very well.
But what was as strange
  In so weak a condition,
As he could not give fees
  He could get no physician.

What wonder he died!
  Yet 't is said that his death
Was occasioned at last
  By the loss of his breath.
But peace to his bones
  Which in ashes now moulder.
Had he lived a day longer
  He 'd have been a day older.

Anonymous.

A CHRONICLE

ONCE — but no matter when —
  There lived — no matter where —
A man, whose name — but then
I need not that declare.

He — well, he had been born,
  And so he was alive;
His age — I details scorn —
  Was somethingty and five.

He lived — how many years
    I truly can't decide;
But this one fact appears
    He lived — until he died.

"He died," I have averred,
    But cannot prove 't was so,
But that he was interred,
    At any rate, I know.

I fancy he'd a son,
    I hear he had a wife:
Perhaps he'd more than one,
    I know not, on my life!

But whether he was rich,
    Or whether he was poor,
Or neither — both — or which,
    I cannot say, I'm sure.

I can't recall his name,
    Or what he used to do:
But then — well, such is fame!
    'T will so serve me and you.

And that is why I thus,
    About this unknown man
Would fain create a fuss,
    To rescue, if I can.

From dark oblivion's blow,
  Some record of his lot:
But, ah! I do not know
  Who — where — when — why — or what.

MORAL

In this brief pedigree
  A moral we should find —
But what it ought to be
  Has quite escaped my mind!

Anonymous.

ON THE OXFORD CARRIER

Here lieth one, who did most truly prove
  That he could never die while he could move;
So hung his destiny never to rot
While he might still jog on and keep his trot;
Made of sphere metal, never to decay
Until his revolution was at stay.
Time numbers motion, yet (without a crime
'Gainst old truth) motion number'd out his time,
And like an engine moved with wheel and weight,
His principles being ceased, he ended straight.
Rest, that gives all men life, gave him his death,
And too much breathing put him out of breath;
Nor were it contradiction to affirm,
Too long vacation hasten'd on his term.

Merely to drive the time away he sicken'd,
Fainted, and died, nor would with ale be quicken'd;
"Nay," quoth he, on his swooning bed outstretch'd,
"If I may n't carry, sure I'll ne'er be fetch'd,
But vow, though the cross doctors all stood hearers,
For one carrier put down to make six bearers."
Ease was his chief disease; and to judge right,
He died for heaviness that his cart went light:
His leisure told him that his time was come,
And lack of load made his life burdensome.
That even to his last breath (there be that say't),
As he were press'd to death, he cried, "More weight;"
But, had his doings lasted as they were,
He had been an immortal carrier.
Obedient to the moon he spent his date
In course reciprocal, and had his fate
Link'd to the mutual flowing of the seas,
Yet (strange to think) his wane was his increase:
His letters are deliver'd all, and gone,
Only remains the superscription.

John Milton.

NEPHELIDIA

FROM the depth of the dreamy decline of the dawn through a notable nimbus of nebulous noonshine,
Pallid and pink as the palm of the flag-flower that flickers with fear of the flies as they float,

Are they looks of our lovers that lustrously lean from a marvel of mystic miraculous moonshine,
These that we feel in the blood of our blushes that thicken and threaten with sobs from the throat?
Thicken and thrill as a theatre thronged at appeal of an actor's appalled agitation,
Fainter with fear of the fires of the future than pale with the promise of pride in the past;
Flushed with the famishing fulness of fever that reddens with radiance of rathe recreation,
Gaunt as the ghastliest of glimpses that gleam through the gloom of the gloaming when ghosts go aghast?
Nay, for the nick of the tick of the time is a tremulous touch on the temples of terror,
Strained as the sinews yet strenuous with strife of the dead who is dumb as the dust-heaps of death:
Surely no soul is it, sweet as the spasm of erotic emotional exquisite error,
Bathed in the balms of beatified bliss, beatific itself by beatitude's breath.
Surely no spirit or sense of a soul that was soft to the spirit and soul of our senses
Sweetens the stress of suspiring suspicion that sobs in the semblance and sound of a sigh;
Only this oracle opens Olympian, in mystical moods and triangular tenses —
Life is the lust of a lamp for the light that is dark till the dawn of the day when we die.

Mild is the mirk and monotonous music of memory melodiously mute as it may be,
While the hope in the heart of a hero is bruised by the breach of men's rapiers resigned to the rod;
Made meek as a mother whose bosom-beats bound with the bliss-bringing bulk of a balm-breathing baby,
As they grope through the grave-yards of creeds, under skies growing green at a groan for the grimness of God.
Blank is the book of his bounty beholden of old and its binding is blacker than bluer:
Out of blue into black is the scheme of the skies, and their dews are the wine of the bloodshed of things;
Till the darkling desire of delight shall be free as a fawn that is freed from the fangs that pursue her,
Till the heart-beats of hell shall be hushed by a hymn from the hunt that has harried the kernel of kings.

A. C. Swinburne,
in " The Heptalogia."

MARTIN LUTHER AT POTSDAM

WHAT lightning shall light it? What thunder shall tell it?
In the height of the height, in the depth of the deep?

Shall the sea-storm declare it, or paint it, or smell it?
  Shall the price of a slave be its treasure to keep?
When the night has grown near with the gems on her bosom,
  When the white of mine eyes is the whiteness of snow,
When the cabman — in liquor — drives a blue roan, a kicker,
  Into the land of the dear long ago.

Ah! — Ah, again! — You will come to me, fall on me —
  You are *so* heavy, and I am *so* flat.
And I? I shall not be at home when you call on me,
  But stray down the wind like a gentleman's hat:
I shall list to the stars when the music is purple,
  Be drawn through a pipe, and exhaled into rings;
Turn to sparks, and then straightway get stuck in the gateway
  That stands between speech and unspeakable things.

As I mentioned before, by what light is it lighted?
  Oh! Is it fourpence, or piebald, or gray?
Is it a mayor that a mother has knighted,
  Or is it a horse of the sun and the day?

Is it a pony? If so, who will change it?
  O golfer, be quiet, and mark where it scuds,
And think of its paces — of owners and races —
  Relinquish the links for the study of studs.

Not understood? Take me hence! Take me yonder!
  Take me away to the land of my rest —
There where the Ganges and other gees wander,
  And uncles and antelopes act for the best,
And all things are mixed and run into each other
  In a violet twilight of virtues and sins,
With the church-spires below you and no one to show you
  Where the curate leaves off and the pew-rent begins!

In the black night through the rank grass the snakes peer —
  The cobs and the cobras are partial to grass —
And a boy wanders out with a knowledge of Shakespeare
  That's not often found in a boy of his class,
And a girl wanders out without any knowledge,
  And a bird wanders out, and a cow wanders out,
Likewise one wether, and they wander together —
  There's a good deal of wandering lying about.

But it's all for the best; I've been told by my friends, Sir,
  That in verses I'd written the meaning was slight;

I've tried with no meaning — to make 'em amends, Sir —
   And find that this kind's still more easy to write.
The title has nothing to do with the verses,
   But think of the millions — the laborers who
In busy employment find deepest enjoyment,
   And yet, like my title, have nothing to do!

Barry Pain.

COMPANIONS

I KNOW not of what we ponder'd
   Or made pretence to talk,
As, her hand within mine, we wander'd
   Tow'rd the pool by the limetree walk,
While the dew fell in showers from the passion flowers
   And the blush-rose bent on her stalk.

I cannot recall her figure:
   Was it regal as Juno's own?
Or only a trifle bigger
   Than the elves who surround the throne
Of the Faëry Queen, and are seen, I ween,
   By mortals in dreams alone?

What her eyes were like, I know not:
   Perhaps they were blurred with tears;
And perhaps in your skies there glow not

(On the contrary) clearer spheres.
No! as to her eyes I am just as wise
  As you or the cat, my dears.

Her teeth, I presume, were "pearly":
  But which was she, brunette or blonde?
Her hair, was it quaintly curly,
  Or as straight as a beadle's wand?
That I failed to remark; — it was rather dark
  And shadowy round the pond.

Then the hand that reposed so snugly
  In mine — was it plump or spare?
Was the countenance fair or ugly?
  Nay, children, you have me there!
My eyes were p'raps blurr'd; and besides, I'd heard
  That it's horribly rude to stare.

And I — was I brusque and surly?
  Or oppressively bland and fond?
Was I partial to rising early?
  Or why did we twain abscond,
All breakfastless too, from the public view
  To prowl by a misty pond?

What passed, what was felt or spoken —
  Whether anything passed at all —
And whether the heart was broken
  That beat under that sheltering shawl —
(If shawl she had on, which I doubt) — has gone
  Yes, gone from me past recall.

Was I haply the lady's suitor?
  Or her uncle? I can't make out —
Ask your governess, dears, or tutor.
  For myself, I'm in hopeless doubt
As to why we were there, and who on earth we were,
  And what this is all about.

C. S. Calverley.

THE COCK AND THE BULL

YOU see this pebble-stone? It's a thing I bought
  Of a bit of a chit of a boy i' the mid o' the day —
I like to dock the smaller parts-o-speech,
As we curtail the already cur-tailed cur
(You catch the paronomasia, play 'po' words?)
Did, rather, i' the pre-Landseerian days.
Well, to my muttons. I purchased the concern,
And clapt it i' my poke, having given for same
By way o' chop, swop, barter or exchange —
"Chop" was my snickering dandiprat's own term —
One shilling and fourpence, current coin o' the realm.
O-n-e one and f-o-u-r four
Pence, one and fourpence — you are with me, sir? —

What hour it skills not: ten or eleven o' the clock,
One day (and what a roaring day it was
Go shop or sight-see — bar a spit o' rain!)
In February, eighteen sixty nine,
Alexandrina Victoria, Fidei,
Hm — hm — how runs the jargon? being on the throne.

Such, sir, are all the facts, succinctly put,
The basis or substratum — what you will —
Of the impending eighty thousand lines.
" Not much in 'em either," quoth perhaps simple Hodge.
But there's a superstructure. Wait a bit.

Mark first the rationale of the thing:
Hear logic rivel and levigate the deed.
That shilling — and for matter o' that, the pence —
I had o' course upo' me — wi' me say —
(*Mecum* 's the Latin, make a note o' that)
When I popp'd pen i' stand, scratched ear, wiped snout,
(Let everybody wipe his own himself)
Sniff'd — tch! — at snuffbox; tumbled up, he-heed,
Haw-haw'd (not he-haw'd, that's another guess thing):
Then fumbled at, and stumbled out of, door,
I shoved the timber ope wi' my omoplat;
And *in vestibulo*, i' the lobby to-wit,
(Iacobi Facciolati's rendering, sir,)
Donned galligaskins, antigropeloes,

A Nonsense Anthology

And so forth; and, complete with hat and gloves,
One on and one a-dangle i' my hand,
And ombrifuge (Lord love you!) cas o' rain,
I flopped forth, 'sbuddikins! on my own ten toes,
(I do assure you there be ten of them)
And went clump-clumping up hill and down dale
To find myself o' the sudden i' front o' the boy.
Put case I had n't 'em on me, could I ha' bought
This sort-o'-kind-o'-what-you-might-call-toy,
This pebble-thing, o' the boy-thing? Q. E. D.
That's proven without aid for mumping Pope,
Sleek porporate or bloated cardinal.
(Is n't it, old Fatchops? You're in Euclid now.)
So, having the shilling — having i' fact a lot —
And pence and halfpence, ever so many o' them,
I purchased, as I think I said before,
The pebble (*lapis, lapidis, di, dem, de* —
What nouns 'crease short i' the genitive, Fatchops, eh?)
O the boy, a bare-legg'd beggarly son of a gun,
For one-and-fourpence. Here we are again.
Now Law steps in, biwigged, voluminous-jaw'd;
Investigates and re-investigates.
Was the transaction illegal? Law shakes head.
Perpend, sir, all the bearings of the case.

At first the coin was mine, the chattel his.
But now (by virtue of the said exchange
And barter) *vice versa* all the coin,
Per juris operationem, vests
I' the boy and his assigns till ding o' doom;

In sæcula sæculo-o-o-orum;
(I think I hear the Abate mouth out that.)
To have and hold the same to him and them . . .
Confer some idiot on Conveyancing.
Whereas the pebble and every part thereof,
And all that appertaineth thereunto,
Quodcunque pertinet ad em rem,
(I fancy, sir, my Latin's rather pat)
Or shall, will, may, might, can, could, would, or should,
Subaudi cætera — clap we to the close —
For what's the good of law in such a case o' the kind
Is mine to all intents and purposes.
This settled, I resume the thread o' the tale.

Now for a touch o' the vendor's quality.
He says a gen'lman bought a pebble of him,
(This pebble i' sooth, sir, which I hold i' m' hand) —
And paid for 't, *like* a gen'lman, on the nail.
"Did I o'ercharge him a ha'penny? Devil a bit
Fiddlepin's end! Get out, you blazing ass!
Gabble o' the goose. Don't bugaboo-baby *me!*
Go double or quits? Yah! tittup! what's the odds?"
— There's the transaction viewed in the vendor's light.

Next ask that dumpled hag, stood snuffling by,
With her three frowsy blowsy brats o' babes,

The scum o' the Kennel, cream o' the filth-heap —
    Faugh !
Aie, aie, aie, aie ! ὀτοτοτοτοτοῖ,
('Stead which we blurt out, Hoighty toighty now) —
And the baker and candlestick maker, and Jack
    and Gill,
Blear'd Goody this and queasy Gaffer that,
Ask the Schoolmaster, Take Schoolmaster first.
He saw a gentleman purchase of a lad
A stone, and pay for it *rite* on the square,
And carry it off *per saltum*, jauntily
Propria quæ maribus, gentleman's property now
    Agreeable to the law explained above).
In proprium usum, for his private ends,
The boy he chucked a brown i' the air, and bit
' the face the shilling ; heaved a thumping stone
At a lean hen that ran cluck-clucking by,
And hit her, dead as nail i' post o' door,)
Then *abiit* — What's the Ciceronian phrase ?
Excessit, evasit, erupit — off slogs boy ;
Off like bird, *avi similis* — (you observed
The dative ? Pretty i' the Mantuan !) — *Anglice*
Off in three flea skips. *Hactenus*, so far,
So good, *tam bene. Bene, satis, male*, —
Where was I with my trope 'bout one in a quag ?
I did once hitch the Syntax into verse
Verbum personale, a verb personal,
Concordat — ay, " agrees," old Fatchops — *cum*
Nominativo, with its nominative,
Genere, i' point of gender, *numero*,
O' number, *et persona*, and person. *Ut*,
Instance : *Sol ruit*, down flops sun, *et* and,

Montes umbrantur, out flounce mountains.   Pah!
Excuse me, sir, I think I 'm going mad.

You see the trick on 't, though, and can yourself
Continue the discourse *ad libitum*.
It takes up about eighty thousand lines,
A thing imagination boggles at;
And might, odds-bobs, sir! in judicious hands
Extend from here to Mesopotamy.

C. S. Calverley.

LOVERS AND A REFLECTION

IN moss-prankt dells which the sunbeams flatter
   (And heaven it knoweth what that may
      mean;
Meaning, however, is no great matter)
   Where woods are a-tremble with words a-tween

Thro' God's own heather we wonned together,
   I and my Willie (O love my love):
I need hardly remark it was glorious weather,
   And flitter-bats wavered alow, above:

Boats were curtseying, rising, bowing,
   (Boats in that climate are so polite,)
And sands were a ribbon of green endowing,
   And O the sun-dazzle on bark and bight!

Thro' the rare red heather we danced together
  (O love my Willie,) and smelt for flowers :
I must mention again it was glorious weather,
  Rhymes are so scarce in this world of ours :

By rises that flushed with their purple favors,
  Thro' becks that brattled o'er grasses sheen,
We walked or waded, we two young shavers,
  Thanking our stars we were both so green.

We journeyed in parallels, I and Willie,
  In fortunate parallels! Butterflies,
Hid in weltering shadows of daffodilly
  Or marjoram, kept making peacock eyes :

Song-birds darted about, some inky
  As coal, some snowy (I ween) as curds ;
Or rosy as pinks, or as roses pinky —
  They reek of no eerie To-come, those birds !

But they skim over bents which the mill-stream washes,
  Or hang in the lift 'neath a white cloud's hem ;
They need no parasols, no goloshes ;
  And good Mrs. Trimmer she feedeth them.

Then we thrid God's cowslips (as erst his heather),
  That endowed the wan grass with their golden blooms;
And snapt— (it was perfectly charming weather) —
  Our fingers at Fate and her goddess-glooms :

And Willie 'gan sing — (Oh, his notes were fluty;
  Wafts fluttered them out to the white-winged sea) —
Something made up of rhymes that have done much duty,
  Rhymes (better to put it) of "ancientry":

Bowers of flowers encountered showers
  In William's carol — (O love my Willie!)
Then he bade sorrow borrow from blithe to-morrow
  I quite forget what — say a daffodilly.

A nest in a hollow, "with buds to follow,"
  I think occurred next in his nimble strain;
And clay that was "kneaden" of course in Eden —
  A rhyme most novel I do maintain:

Mists, bones, the singer himself, love-stories,
  And all least furlable things got furled;
Not with any design to conceal their glories,
  But simply and solely to rhyme with world.

O if billows and pillows and hours and flowers,
  And all the brave rhymes of an elder day,
Could be furled together, this genial weather,
  And carted or carried on wafts away,
Nor ever again trotted out — ah me!
How much fewer volumes of verse there 'd be.

C. S. Calverley.

AN IMITATION OF WORDSWORTH

THERE is a river clear and fair,
    'T is neither broad nor narrow;
   It winds a little here and there —
It winds about like any hare;
And then it takes as straight a course
As on the turnpike road a horse,
  Or through the air an arrow.

The trees that grow upon the shore,
Have grown a hundred years or more;
    So long there is no knowing.
Old Daniel Dobson does not know
When first these trees began to grow;
But still they grew, and grew, and grew,
As if they 'd nothing else to do,
  But ever to be growing.

The impulses of air and sky
Have rear'd their stately heads so high,
  And clothed their boughs with green;
Their leaves the dews of evening quaff, —
  And when the wind blows loud and keen,
I 've seen the jolly timbers laugh,
  And shake their sides with merry glee —
  Wagging their heads in mockery.

Fix'd are their feet in solid earth,
   Where winds can never blow;
But visitings of deeper birth
   Have reach'd their roots below.
For they have gain'd the river's brink,
And of the living waters drink.

There's little Will, a five years child —
   He is my youngest boy:
To look on eyes so fair and wild,
   It is a very joy: —
He hath conversed with sun and shower,
And dwelt with every idle flower,
   As fresh and gay as them.
He loiters with the briar rose, —
The blue-belles are his play-fellows,
   That dance upon their slender stem.

And I have said, my little Will,
Why should not he continue still
   A thing of Nature's rearing?
A thing beyond the world's control —
A living vegetable soul, —
   No human sorrow fearing.

It were a blessed sight to see
That child become a Willow-tree,
   His brother trees among.
He'd be four times as tall as me,
   And live three times as long.

Catharine M. Fanshawe.

THE FAMOUS BALLAD OF THE JUBILEE CUP

YOU may lift me up in your arms, lad, and turn my face to the sun,
    For a last look back at the dear old track where the Jubilee cup was won;
And draw your chair to my side, lad — no, thank ye, I feel no pain —
For I'm going out with the tide, lad; but I'll tell you the tale again.

I'm seventy-nine or nearly, and my head it has long turned gray,
But it all comes back as clearly as though it was yesterday —
The dust, and the bookies shouting around the clerk of the scales,
And the clerk of the course, and the nobs in force, and 'Is 'Ighness the Pr**ce of W*les.

T was a nine-hole thresh to wind'ard (but none of us cared for that),
With a straight run home to the service tee, and a finish along the flat,
"Stiff?" ah, well you may say it! Spot barred, and at five stone ten!
But at two and a bisque I'd ha' run the risk; for I was a greenhorn then.

So we stripped to the B. Race signal, the old red
 swallowtail —
There was young Ben Bolt and the Portland Colt,
 and Aston Villa, and Yale;
And W. G., and Steinitz, Leander and The Saint,
And the G*rm*n Emp*r*r's Meteor, a-looking as
 fresh as paint;

John Roberts (scratch), and Safety Match, The
 Lascar, and Lorna Doone,
Oom Paul (a bye), and Romany Rye, and me upon
 Wooden Spoon;
And some of us cut for partners, and some of us
 strung for baulk,
And some of us tossed for stations — But there,
 what use to talk?

Three-quarter-back on the Kingsclere crack was
 station enough for me,
With a fresh jackyarder blowing and the Vicarage
 goal a-lee!
And I leaned and patted her centre-bit and eased
 the quid in her cheek,
With a "Soh my lass!" and a "Woa you brute!"
 — for she could do all but speak.

She was geared a thought too high perhaps; she
 was trained a trifle fine;
But she had the grand reach forward! I never saw
 such a line!

Smooth-bored, clean run, from her fiddle head with
    its dainty ear half-cock,
Hard-bit, *pur sang*, from her overhang to the heel
    of her off hind sock.

Sir Robert he walked beside me as I worked her
    down to the mark ;
" There 's money on this, my lad," said he, " and
    most of 'em 's running dark ;
But ease the sheet if you 're bunkered, and pack
    the scrummages tight,
And use your slide at the distance, and we 'll drink
    to your health to-night ! "

But I bent and tightened my stretcher. Said I to
    myself, said I —
" John Jones, this here is the Jubilee Cup, and
    you have to do or die."
And the words were n't hardly spoken when the
    umpire shouted " Play ! "
And we all kicked off from the Gasworks End with
    a " Yoicks ! " and a " Gone Away ! "

And at first I thought of nothing, as the clay flew
    by in lumps,
But stuck to the old Ruy Lopez, and wondered
    who 'd call for trumps,
And luffed her close to the cushion, and watched
    each one as it broke,
And in triple file up the Rowley Mile we went like
    a trail of smoke.

The Lascar made the running but he did n't
    amount to much,
For old Oom Paul was quick on the ball, and
    headed it back to touch;
And the whole first flight led off with the right as
    The Saint took up the pace,
And drove it clean to the putting green and
    trumped it there with an ace.

John Roberts had given a miss in baulk, but Villa
    cleared with a punt;
And keeping her service hard and low the Meteor
    forged to the front;
With Romany Rye to windward at dormy and two
    to play,
And Yale close up — but a Jubilee Cup is n't run
    for every day.

We laid our course for the Warner — I tell you
    the pace was hot!
And again off Tattenham Corner a blanket covered
    the lot.
Check side! Check side! now steer her wide! and
    barely an inch of room,
With The Lascar's tail over our lee rail and brush-
    ing Leander's boom.

We were running as strong as ever — eight knots
    — but it could n't last;
For the spray and the bails were flying, the whole
    field tailing fast;

And the Portland Colt had shot his bolt, and Yale
  was bumped at the Doves,
And The Lascar resigned to Steinitz, stalemated in
  fifteen moves.

It was bellows to mend with Roberts — starred
  three for a penalty kick:
But he chalked his cue and gave 'em the butt, and
  Oom Paul marked the trick —
"Offside — No Ball — and at fourteen all! Mark
  Cock! and two for his nob!"
When W. G. ran clean through his lee and beat
  him twice with a lob.

He yorked him twice on a crumbling pitch and
  wiped his eye with a brace,
But his guy-rope split with the strain of it and he
  dropped back out of the race;
And I drew a bead on the Meteor's lead, and
  challenging none too soon,
Bent over and patted her garboard strake, and
  called upon Wooden Spoon.

She was all of a shiver forward, the spoondrift thick
  on her flanks,
But I'd brought her an easy gambit, and nursed
  her over the banks;
She answered her helm — the darling! and woke
  up now with a rush,
While the Meteor's jock, he sat like a rock — he
  knew we rode for his brush!

There was no one else left in it. The Saint was
 using his whip,
And Safety Match, with a lofting catch, was
 pocketed deep at slip;
And young Ben Bolt with his niblick took miss at
 Leander's lunge,
But topped the net with the ricochet, and Steinitz
 threw up the sponge.

But none of the lot could stop the rot — nay, don't
 ask *me* to stop!
The villa had called for lemons, Oom Paul had
 taken his drop,
And both were kicking the referee. Poor fellow!
 he done his best;
But, being in doubt, he'd ruled them out — which
 he always did when pressed.

So, inch by inch, I tightened the winch, and
 chucked the sandbags out —
I heard the nursery cannons pop, I heard the
 bookies shout:
" The Meteor wins!" " No, Wooden Spoon!"
 " Check!" " Vantage!" " Leg Before!"
" Last Lap!" " Pass Nap!" At his saddle-flap I
 put up the helm and wore.

You may overlap at the saddle-flap, and yet be
 loo'd on the tape:
And it all depends upon changing ends, how a
 seven-year-old will shape;

A Nonsense Anthology

It was tack and tack to the Lepe and back — a fair ding-dong to the Ridge,
And he led by his forward canvas yet as we shot 'neath Hammersmith Bridge.

He led by his forward canvas — he led from his strongest suit —
But along we went on a roaring scent, and at Fawley I gained a foot.
He fisted off with his jigger, and gave me his wash — too late!
Deuce — Vantage — Check! By neck and neck we rounded into the straight.

I could hear the "Conquering 'Ero" a-crashing on Godfrey's band,
And my hopes fell sudden to zero, just there, with the race in hand —
In sight of the Turf's Blue Ribbon, in sight of the umpire's tape,
As I felt the tack of her spinnaker c-rack! as I heard the steam escape!

Had I lost at that awful juncture my presence of mind? . . . but no!
I leaned and felt for the puncture, and plugged it there with my toe . . .
Hand over hand by the Members' Stand I lifted and eased her up,
Shot — clean and fair — to the crossbar there, and landed the Jubilee Cup!

"The odd by a head, and leg before," so the Judge
    he gave the word:
And the umpire shouted "Over!" but I neither
    spoke nor stirred.
They crowded round: for there on the ground I
    lay in a dead-cold swoon,
Pitched neck and crop on the turf atop of my
    beautiful Wooden Spoon.

Her dewlap tire was punctured, her bearings all red
    hot;
She'd a lolling tongue, and her bowsprit sprung,
    and her running gear in a knot;
And amid the sobs of her backers, Sir Robert
    loosened her girth
And led her away to the knacker's. She had raced
    her last on earth!

But I mind me well of the tear that fell from the
    eye of our noble Pr*nce,
And the things he said as he tucked me in bed —
    and I've lain there ever since;
Tho' it all gets mixed up queerly that happened
    before my spill, —
But I draw my thousand yearly: it'll pay for the
    doctor's bill.

I'm going out with the tide, lad — you'll dig me
    a numble grave,
And whiles you will bring your bride, lad, and your
    sons, if sons you have,

And there when the dews are weeping, and the echoes murmur "Peace!"
And the salt, salt tide comes creeping and covers the popping-crease;

In the hour when the ducks deposit their eggs with a boasted force,
They'll look and whisper "How was it?" and you'll take them over the course,
And your voice will break as you try to speak of the glorious first of June,
When the Jubilee Cup, with John Jones up, was won upon Wooden Spoon.

Arthur T. Quiller-Couch.

A SONG OF IMPOSSIBILITIES

LADY, I loved you all last year,
  How honestly and well —
  Alas! would weary you to hear,
  And torture me to tell;
I raved beneath the midnight sky,
  I sang beneath the limes —
Orlando in my lunacy,
  And Petrarch in my rhymes.
But all is over! When the sun
  Dries up the boundless main,
When black is white, false-hearted one,
  I may be yours again!

When passion's early hopes and fears
  Are not derided things;
When truth is found in falling tears,
  Or faith in golden rings;
When the dark Fates that rule our way
  Instruct me where they hide
One woman that would ne'er betray,
  One friend that never lied;
When summer shines without a cloud,
  And bliss without a pain;
When worth is noticed in a crowd,
  I may be yours again!

When science pours the light of day
  Upon the lords of lands;
When Huskisson is heard to say
  That Lethbridge understands;
When wrinkles work their way in youth,
  Or Eldon's in a hurry;
When lawyers represent the truth,
  Or Mr. Sumner Surrey;
When aldermen taste eloquence
  Or bricklayers champagne;
When common law is common sense,
  I may be yours again!

When learned judges play the beau,
  Or learned pigs the tabor;
When traveller Bankes beats Cicero,
  Or Mr. Bishop Weber;
When sinking funds discharge a debt,
  Or female hands a bomb;

When bankrupts study the *Gazette*,
  Or colleges *Tom Thumb*;
When little fishes learn to speak,
  Or poets not to feign;
When Dr. Geldart construes Greek,
  I may be yours again!

When Pole and Thornton honor cheques,
  Or Mr. Const a rogue;
When Jericho 's in Middlesex,
  Or minuets in vogue;
When Highgate goes to Devonport,
  Or fashion to Guildhall;
When argument is heard at Court,
  Or Mr. Wynn at all;
When Sydney Smith forgets to jest,
  Or farmers to complain;
When kings that are are not the best,
  I may be yours again!

When peers from telling money shrink,
  Or monks from telling lies;
When hydrogen begins to sink,
  Or Grecian scrip to rise;
When German poets cease to dream,
  Americans to guess;
When Freedom sheds her holy beam
  On Negroes, and the Press;
When there is any fear of Rome,
  Or any hope of Spain;
When Ireland is a happy home,
  I may be yours again!

When you can cancel what has been,
    Or alter what must be,
Or bring once more that vanished scene,
    Those withered joys to me;
When you can tune the broken lute,
    Or deck the blighted wreath,
Or rear the garden's richest fruit,
    Upon a blasted heath;
When you can lure the wolf at bay
    Back to his shattered chain,
To-day may then be yesterday —
    I may be yours again!

W. M. Praed.

TRUST IN WOMEN

*When these things following be done to our intent,
Then put women in trust and confident.*

WHEN nettles in winter bring forth roses red,
    And all manner of thorn trees bear figs naturally,
And geese bear pearls in every mead,
    And laurel bear cherries abundantly,
    And oaks bear dates very plenteously,
And kisks give of honey superfluence,
Then put women in trust and confidence.

A Nonsense Anthology

When box bear paper in every land and town,
    And thistles bear berries in every place,
And pikes have naturally feathers in their crown,
    And bulls of the sea sing a good bass,
    And men be the ships fishes trace,
And in women be found no insipience,
Then put them in trust and confidence.

When whitings do walk forests to chase harts,
    And herrings their horns in forests boldly blow,
And marmsets mourn in moors and lakes,
    And gurnards shoot rooks out of a crossbow,
    And goslings hunt the wolf to overthrow,
And sprats bear spears in armès of defence,
Then put women in trust and confidence.

When swine be cunning in all points of music,
    And asses be doctors of every science,
And cats do heal men by practising of physic,
    And buzzards to scripture give any credence,
    And merchants buy with horn, instead of groats and pence,
And pyes be made poets for their eloquence,
Then put women in trust and confidence.

When sparrows build churches on a height,
    And wrens carry sacks unto the mill,
And curlews carry timber houses to dight,
    And fomalls bear butter to market to sell,
    And woodcocks bear woodknives cranes to kill,
And greenfinches to goslings do obedience,
Then put women in trust and confidence.

When crows take salmon in woods and parks,
   And be take with swifts and snails,
And camels in the air take swallows and larks,
   And mice move mountains by wagging of their
      tails,
   And shipmen take a ride instead of sails,
And when wives to their husbands do no offence,
Then put women in trust and confidence.

When antelopes surmount eagles in flight,
   And swans be swifter than hawks of the tower,
And wrens set gos-hawks by force and might,
   And muskets make verjuice of crabbes sour,
   And ships sail on dry land, silt give flower,
And apes in Westminster give judgment and
      sentence,
Then put women in trust and confidence.

Anonymous

HERE IS THE TALE

After Rudyard Kipling

Here is the tale — and you must make the most of it
   Here is the rhyme — ah, listen and attend!
Backwards — forwards — read it all and boast of it
   If you are anything the wiser at the end!

NOW Jack looked up — it was time to sup
   and the bucket was yet to fill,
   And Jack looked round for a space and
      frowned, then beckoned his sister Jill.

A Nonsense Anthology

And twice he pulled his sister's hair, and thrice he smote her side;
"Ha' done, ha' done with your impudent fun — ha' done with your games!" she cried;
"You have made mud-pies of a marvellous size — finger and face are black,
You have trodden the Way of the Mire and Clay — now up and wash you, Jack!
Or else, or ever we reach our home, there waiteth an angry dame —
Well you know the weight of her blow — the supperless open shame!
Wash, if you will, on yonder hill — wash, if you will, at the spring, —
Or keep your dirt, to your certain hurt, and an imminent walloping!"

"You must wash — you must scrub — you must scrape!" growled Jack, "you must traffic with cans and pails,
Nor keep the spoil of the good brown soil in the rim of your finger-nails!
The morning path you must tread to your bath — you must wash ere the night descends,
And all for the cause of conventional laws and the soapmakers' dividends!
But if 't is sooth that our meal in truth depends on our washing, Jill,
By the sacred right of our appetite — haste — haste to the top of the hill!"

They have trodden the Way of the Mire and Clay
    they have toiled and travelled far,
They have climbed to the brow of the hill-top now
    where the bubbling fountains are,
They have taken the bucket and filled it up — yea
    filled it up to the brim;
But Jack he sneered at his sister Jill, and Jill she
    jeered at him:
"What, blown already!" Jack cried out (and his
    was a biting mirth!)
"You boast indeed of your wonderful speed — but
    what is the boasting worth?
Now, if you can run as the antelope runs, and if
    you can turn like a hare,
Come, race me, Jill, to the foot of the hill — and
    prove your boasting fair!"

"Race? What is a race" (and a mocking face had
    Jill as she spake the word)
"Unless for a prize the runner tries? The truth
    indeed ye heard,
For I can run as the antelope runs, and I can turn
    like a hare: —
The first one down wins half-a-crown — and I will
    race you there!"
"Yea, if for the lesson that you will learn (the
    lesson of humbled pride)
The price you fix at two-and-six, it shall not be
    denied;
Come, take your stand at my right hand, for here
    is the mark we toe:

Now, are you ready, and are you steady? Gird up
    your petticoats! Go!"

And Jill she ran like a winging bolt, a bolt from
    the bow released,
But Jack like a stream of the lightning gleam, with
    its pathway duly greased;
He ran down hill in front of Jill like a summer-
    lightning flash —
Till he suddenly tripped on a stone, or slipped, and
    fell to the earth with a crash.
Then straight did rise on his wondering eyes the
    constellations fair,
Arcturus and the Pleiades, the Greater and Lesser
    Bear,
The swirling rain of a comet's train he saw, as he
    swiftly fell —
And Jill came tumbling after him with a loud
    triumphant yell:
"You have won, you have won, the race is done!
    And as for the wager laid —
You have fallen down with a broken crown — the
    half-crown debt is paid!"

They have taken Jack to the room at the back
    where the family medicines are,
And he lies in bed with a broken head in a halo of
    vinegar;
While, in that Jill had laughed her fill as her
    brother fell to earth,
She had felt the sting of a walloping — she hath
    paid the price of her mirth!

Here is the tale — and now you have the whole of it,
Here is the story — well and wisely planned,
Beauty — Duty — these make up the soul of it —
But, ah, my little readers, will you mark and understand?

Anthony C. Deane.

THE AULD WIFE

THE auld wife sat at her ivied door,
    (Butter and eggs and a pound of cheese)
  A thing she had frequently done before;
And her spectacles lay on her aproned knees.

The piper he piped on the hill-top high,
    (Butter and eggs and a pound of cheese)
Till the cow said "I die" and the goose asked "Why;"
And the dog said nothing, but searched for fleas.

The farmer he strode through the square farmyard;
    (Butter and eggs and a pound of cheese)
His last brew of ale was a trifle hard,
  The connection of which with the plot one sees.

The farmer's daughter hath frank blue eyes,
    (Butter and eggs and a pound of cheese)
She hears the rooks caw in the windy skies,
  As she sits at her lattice and shells her peas.

The farmer's daughter hath ripe red lips;
   (Butter and eggs and a pound of cheese)
If you try to approach her, away she skips
   Over tables and chairs with apparent ease.

The farmer's daughter hath soft brown hair;
   (Butter and eggs and a pound of cheese)
And I met with a ballad, I can't say where,
   Which wholly consisted of lines like these.

She sat with her hands 'neath her dimpled cheeks,
   (Butter and eggs and a pound of cheese)
And spake not a word. While a lady speaks
   There is hope, but she did n't even sneeze.

She sat with her hands 'neath her crimson cheeks;
   (Butter and eggs and a pound of cheese)
She gave up mending her father's breeks,
   And let the cat roll in her best chemise.

She sat with her hands 'neath her burning cheeks
   (Butter and eggs and a pound of cheese),
And gazed at the piper for thirteen weeks;
   Then she followed him out o'er the misty leas.

Her sheep followed her as their tails did them
   (Butter and eggs and a pound of cheese),
And this song is considered a perfect gem,
   And as to the meaning, it's what you please.

Charles S. Calverley.

NOT I

SOME like drink
   In a pint pot,
  Some like to think,
Some not.

Strong Dutch cheese,
  Old Kentucky Rye,
Some like these;
  Not I.

Some like Poe,
  And others like Scott;
Some like Mrs. Stowe,
  Some not.

Some like to laugh,
  Some like to cry,
Some like to chaff;
  Not I.

R. L. Stevenson.

MINNIE AND WINNIE

MINNIE and Winnie
  Slept in a shell.
  Sleep, little ladies!
And they slept well.

Pink was the shell within,
    Silver without;
Sounds of the great sea
    Wandered about.

Sleep little ladies!
    Wake not soon!
Echo on echo
    Dies to the moon.

Two bright stars
    Peep'd into the shell,
What are they dreaming of?
    Who can tell?

Started a green linnet
    Out of the croft;
Wake, little ladies,
    The sun is aloft!

Lord Tennyson.

THE MAYOR OF SCUTTLETON*

THE Mayor of Scuttleton burned his nose
    Trying to warm his copper toes;
He lost his money and spoiled his will
By signing his name with an icicle quill;
He went bareheaded, and held his breath,
And frightened his grandame most to death;
He loaded a shovel and tried to shoot,
And killed the calf in the leg of his boot;

* From "Rhymes and Jingles," copyright, 1874, 1902, Charles Scribner's Sons.

He melted a snowbird and formed the habit
Of dancing jigs with a sad Welsh rabbit;
He lived on taffy and taxed the town;
And read his newspaper upside down;
Then he sighed and hung his hat on a feather,
And bade the townspeople come together;
But the worst of it all was, nobody knew
What the Mayor of Scuttleton next would do.

Mary Mapes Dodge.

THE PURPLE COW *

I NEVER saw a Purple Cow,
   I never hope to see one;
But I can tell you, anyhow,
   I'd rather see than be one.

Gelett Burgess

THE INVISIBLE BRIDGE *

I'D Never Dare to Walk across
   A Bridge I Could Not See;
For Quite afraid of Falling off,
   I fear that I Should Be!

Gelett Burgess

* By permission of Gelett Burgess; from "The Burgess Nonsense Book," copyright, 1901.

THE LAZY ROOF*

THE Roof it has a Lazy Time
    A-lying in the Sun;
  The Walls they have to Hold Him Up;
They do Not Have Much Fun!
Gelett Burgess.

MY FEET*

MY feet, they haul me Round the House,
    They Hoist me up the Stairs;
  I only have to Steer them and
They Ride me Everywheres.
Gelett Burgess.

THE HEN †

ALAS! my Child, where is the Pen
    That can do Justice to the Hen?
  Like Royalty, She goes her way,
Laying foundations every day,
Though not for Public Buildings, yet
For Custard, Cake and Omelette.

---

* By permission of Gelett Burgess; from "The Burgess Nonsense Book," copyright, 1901.
† By permission of Oliver Herford; from "More Animals," copyright, 1901.

Or if too Old for such a use
They have their Fling at some Abuse,
As when to Censure Plays Unfit
Upon the Stage they make a Hit,
Or at elections Seal the Fate
Of an Obnoxious Candidate.
No wonder, Child, we prize the Hen,
Whose Egg is Mightier than the Pen.

Oliver Herford.

THE COW *

THE Cow is too well known, I fear,
    To need an introduction here.
    If She should vanish from earth's face
It would be hard to fill her place;
For with the Cow would disappear
So much that every one holds Dear.
Oh, think of all the Boots and Shoes,
Milk Punches, Gladstone Bags and Stews,
And Things too numerous to count,
Of which, my child, she is the Fount.
Let's hope, at least, the Fount may last
Until *our* Generation's past.

Oliver Herford.

* By permission of Oliver Herford; from "More Animals," copyright, 1901.

THE CHIMPANZEE *

CHILDREN, behold the Chimpanzee:
   He sits on the ancestral tree
   From which we sprang in ages gone.
I'm glad we sprang: had we held on,
We might, for aught that I can say,
Be horrid Chimpanzees to-day.

Oliver Herford.

THE HIPPOPOTAMUS *

"OH, say, what is this fearful, wild,
   Incorrigible cuss?"
   "This *creature* (don't say 'cuss,' my child;
'T is slang) — this creature fierce is styled
The Hippopotamus.
His curious name derives its source
From two Greek words: *hippos* — a horse,
Potamos — river. See?
The river's plain enough, of course;
But why they called *that* thing a *horse*,
That's what is Greek to me."

Oliver Herford.

THE PLATYPUS *

MY child, the Duck-billed Platypus
   A sad example sets for us:
   From him we learn how Indecision
Of character provokes Derision.

---

* By permission of Oliver Herford; from "A Child's Primer of Natural History," copyright, 1899.

This vacillating Thing, you see,
Could not decide which he would be,
Fish, Flesh or Fowl, and chose all three.
The scientists were sorely vexed
To classify him; so perplexed
Their brains, that they, with Rage at bay,
Called him a horrid name one day, —
A name that baffles, frights and shocks us,
Ornithorhynchus Paradoxus.

Oliver Herford.

SOME GEESE *

EV-ER-Y child who has the use
   Of his sen-ses knows a goose.
   See them un-der-neath the tree
Gath-er round the goose-girl's knee,
While she reads them by the hour
From the works of Scho-pen-hau-er.

How pa-tient-ly the geese at-tend!
But do they re-al-ly com-pre-hend
What Scho-pen-hau-er's driv-ing at?
Oh, not at all; but what of that?
Nei-ther do I; nei-ther does she;
And, for that mat-ter, nor does he.

Oliver Herford

---

* By permission of Oliver Herford; from "A Child's Primer of Natural History," copyright, 1899.

THE FLAMINGO*

*Inspired by reading a chorus of spirits
in a German play*

First Voice.

OH! tell me have you ever seen a red, long-leg'd Flamingo?
Oh! tell me have you ever yet seen him the water in go?

Second Voice.

Oh! yes at Bowling-Green I've seen a red long-leg'd Flamingo,
Oh! yes at Bowling-Green I've there seen him the water in go.

First Voice.

Oh! tell me did you ever see a bird so funny stand-o
When forth he from the water comes and gets upon the land-o?

Second Voice.

No! in my life I ne'er did see a bird so funny stand-o
When forth he from the water comes and gets upon the land-o.

* By permission of D. Appleton & Co.

First Voice.

He has a leg some three feet long, or near it, so they say, Sir.
Stiff upon one alone he stands, t' other he stows away, Sir.

Second Voice.

And what an ugly head he's got! I wonder that he'd wear it.
But rather *more* I wonder that his long, thin neck can bear it.

First Voice.

And think, this length of neck and legs (no doubt they have their uses)
Are members of a little frame, much smaller than a goose's!

Both.

Oh! isn't he a curious bird, that red, long-leg'd Flamingo?
A water bird, a gawky bird, a sing'lar bird, by jingo!

Lewis Gaylord Clark.

KINDNESS TO ANIMALS

SPEAK gently to the herring and kindly to the calf,
   Be blithesome with the bunny, at barnacles don't laugh!
Give nuts unto the monkey, and buns unto the bear,
Ne'er hint at currant jelly if you chance to see a hare!
Oh, little girls, pray hide your combs when tortoises draw nigh,
And never in the hearing of a pigeon whisper Pie!
But give the stranded jelly-fish a shove into the sea, —
Be always kind to animals wherever you may be!

Oh, make not game of sparrows, nor faces at the ram,
And ne'er allude to mint sauce when calling on a lamb.
Don't beard the thoughtful oyster, don't dare the cod to crimp,
Don't cheat the pike, or ever try to pot the playful shrimp.
Tread lightly on the turning worm, don't bruise the butterfly,
Don't ridicule the wry-neck, nor sneer at salmon-fry;
Oh, ne'er delight to make dogs fight, nor bantams disagree, —
Be always kind to animals wherever you may be!

Be lenient with lobsters, and ever kind to crabs,
And be not disrespectful to cuttle-fish or dabs;
Chase not the Cochin-China, chaff not the ox obese,
And babble not of feather-beds in company with geese.
Be tender with the tadpole, and let the limpet thrive,
Be merciful to mussels, don't skin your eels alive;
When talking to a turtle don't mention calipee —
Be always kind to animals wherever you may be.

J. Ashby-Sterry.

SAGE COUNSEL

THE lion is the beast to fight,
    He leaps along the plain,
  And if you run with all your might,
He runs with all his mane.
    I'm glad I'm not a Hottentot,
    But if I were, with outward cal-lum
      I'd either faint upon the spot
      Or hie me up a leafy pal-lum.

The chamois is the beast to hunt;
    He's fleeter than the wind,
And when the chamois is in front,
    The hunter is behind.
      The Tyrolese make famous cheese
      And hunt the chamois o'er the chaz-zums;
      I'd choose the former if you please,
      For precipices give me spaz-zums.

The polar bear will make a rug
   Almost as white as snow;
But if he gets you in his hug,
   He rarely lets you go.
      And Polar ice looks very nice,
        With all the colors of a pris-sum;
      But, if you'll follow my advice,
        Stay home and learn your catechissum.

A. T. Quiller-Couch.

OF BAITING THE LION *

REMEMBERING his taste for blood
   You'd better bait him with a cow;
Persuade the brute to chew the cud
   Her tail suspended from a bough;
It thrills the lion through and through
   To hear the milky creature moo.

Having arranged this simple ruse,
   Yourself you climb a neighboring tree;
See to it that the spot you choose
   Commands the coming tragedy;
Take up a smallish Maxim gun,
   A search-light, whisky, and a bun.

It's safer, too, to have your bike
   Standing immediately below,
In case your piece should fail to strike,
   Or deal an ineffective blow;

---

* By permission of John Lane; from "In Cap and Bells," copyright, 1899.

The Lion moves with perfect grace,
   But cannot go the scorcher's pace.

Keep open ear for subtle signs;
   Thus, when the cow profusely moans,
That means to say, the Lion dines.
   The crunching sound, of course, is bones;
Silence resumes her ancient reign —
   This shows the cow is out of pain.

But when a fat and torpid hum
   Escapes the eater's unctuous nose,
Turn up the light and let it come
   Full on his innocent repose;
Then pour your shot between his eyes,
   And go on pouring till he dies.

Play, even so, discretion's part;
   Descend with stealth; bring on your gun;
Then lay your hand above his heart
   To see if he is really done;
Don't skin him till you know he's dead
   Or you may perish in his stead!

Years hence, at home, when talk is tall,
   You'll set the gun-room wide agape,
Describing how with just a small
   Pea-rifle, going after ape
You met a Lion unaware,
   And felled him flying through the air.

Owen Seaman.

THE FROG

BE kind and tender to the Frog,
    And do not call him names,
  As " Slimy-Skin," or " Polly-wog,"
  Or likewise, " Uncle James,"
  Or "Gape-a-grin," or "Toad-gone-wrong,"
  Or " Billy-Bandy-knees ; "
The Frog is justly sensitive
  To epithets like these.

No animal will more repay
  A treatment kind and fair,
At least, so lonely people say
Who keep a frog (and, by the way,
  They are extremely rare).

Hilaire Belloc.

THE YAK

AS a friend to the children commend me the yak,
    You will find it exactly the thing :
  It will carry and fetch, you can ride on its back,
    Or lead it about with a string.

A Tartar who dwells on the plains of Thibet
    (A desolate region of snow)
Has for centuries made it a nursery pet,
    And surely the Tartar should know !

Then tell your papa where the Yak can be got,
    And if he is awfully rich,
He will buy you the creature — or else he will not,
    (I cannot be positive which).

Hilaire Belloc

THE PYTHON

A PYTHON I should not advise, —
    It needs a doctor for its eyes,
        And has the measles yearly.

However, if you feel inclined
To get one (to improve your mind,
    And not from fashion merely),
Allow no music near its cage;
And when it flies into a rage
    Chastise it most severely.

I had an Aunt in Yucatan
Who bought a Python from a man
    And kept it for a pet.
She died because she never knew
These simple little rules and few; —
    The snake is living yet.

Hilaire Belloc

THE BISON

THE Bison is vain, and (I write it with pain)
    The Door-mat you see on his head
  Is not, as some learned professors maintain,
The opulent growth of a genius' brain;
    But is sewn on with needle and thread.

Hilaire Belloc.

THE PANTHER

BE kind to the panther! for when thou wert young,
    In thy country far over the sea,
'T was a panther ate up thy papa and mamma,
    And had several mouthfuls of thee!

Be kind to the badger! for who shall decide
    The depths of his badgerly soul?
And think of the tapir when flashes the lamp
    O'er the fast and the free-flowing bowl.

Be kind to the camel! nor let word of thine
    Ever put up his bactrian back;
And cherish the she-kangaroo with her bag,
    Nor venture to give her the sack.

Be kind to the ostrich! for how canst thou hope
    To have such a stomach as it?
And when the proud day of your bridal shall come,
    Do give the poor birdie a bit.

Be kind to the walrus! nor ever forget
  To have it on Tuesday to tea;
But butter the crumpets on only one side,
  Save such as are eaten by thee.

Be kind to the bison! and let the jackal
  In the light of thy love have a share;
And coax the ichneumon to grow a new tail,
  And have lots of larks in its lair.

Be kind to the bustard! that genial bird,
  And humor its wishes and ways;
And when the poor elephant suffers from bile,
  Then tenderly lace up his stays!

Anonymous.

THE MONKEY'S GLUE

WHEN the monkey in his madness
    Took the glue to mend his voice,
    'T was the crawfish showed his sadness
That the bluebird could rejoice.

Then the perspicacious parrot
  Sought to save the suicide
By administering carrot,
  But the monkey merely died.

So the crawfish and the parrot
  Sauntered slowly toward the sea,
While the bluebird stole the carrot
  And returned the glue to me.

Goldwin Goldsmith.

THERE WAS A FROG

THERE was a frog swum in the lake,
  The crab came crawling by:
  "Wilt thou," coth the frog, "be my make?"
 Coth the crab, "No, not I."
"My skin is sooth and dappled fine,
  I can leap far and nigh.
Thy shell is hard: so is not mine."
 Coth the crab, "No, not I."
"Tell me," then spake the crab, "therefore,
  Or else I thee defy:
Give me thy claw, I ask no more."
 Coth the frog, "That will I."
The crab bit off the frog's fore-feet;
 The frog then he must die.
To woo a crab it is not meet:
 If any do, it is not I.

From Christ Church MS., I. 549.

THE BLOATED BIGGABOON

THE bloated Biggaboon
  Was so haughty, he would not repose
  In a house, or a hall, or *ces choses*,
But he slept his high sleep in his clothes —
   'Neath the moon.

The bloated Biggaboon
Pour'd contempt upon waistcoat and skirt,
Holding swallow-tails even as dirt —
So he puff'd himself out in his shirt,
    Like a b'loon.

H. Cholmondeley-Pennell.

WILD FLOWERS *

"OF what are you afraid, my child?" inquired the kindly teacher.
"Oh, sir! the flowers, they are wild," replied the timid creature.

Peter Newell.

TIMID HORTENSE *

"NOW, if the fish will only bite, we'll have some royal fun."
"And do fish bite? The horrid things! Indeed, I'll not catch one!"

Peter Newell.

HER POLKA DOTS *

SHE played upon her music-box a fancy air by chance,
And straightway all her polka-dots began a lively dance.

Peter Newell.

* By permission of Harper & Brothers; from "Pictures and Rhymes," copyright, 1900.

HER DAIRY *

"A MILKWEED, and a buttercup, and cow-
　　slip," said sweet Mary,
"Are growing in my garden-plot, and this
　　I call my dairy."

Peter Newell.

TURVEY TOP

'TWAS after a supper of Norfolk brawn
　　That into a doze I chanced to drop,
　　And thence awoke in the gray of dawn,
In the wonder-land of Turvey Top.

A land so strange I never had seen,
　　And could not choose but look and laugh —
A land where the small the great includes,
　　And the whole is less than the half!

A land where the circles were not lines
　　Round central points, as schoolmen show,
And the parallels met whenever they chose,
　　And went playing at touch-and-go!

There — except that every round was square
　　And save that all the squares were rounds —
No surface had limits anywhere,
　　So they never could beat the bounds.

* By permission of Harper & Brothers; from "Pictures and Rhymes," copyright, 1900.

In their gardens, fruit before blossom came,
    And the trees diminished as they grew;
And you never went out to walk a mile,
    'T was the mile that walked to you.

The people there are not tall or short,
    Heavy or light, or stout or thin,
And their lives begin where they should leave off,
    Or leave off where they should begin.

There childhood, with naught of childish glee,
    Looks on the world with thoughtful brow;
'T is only the aged who laugh and crow,
    And cry, "We have done with it now!"

A singular race! what lives they spent!
    Got up before they went to bed!
And never a man said what he meant,
    Or a woman meant what she said.

They blended colours that will not blend,
    All hideous contrasts voted sweet;
In yellow and red their Quakers dress'd,
    And considered it rather neat.

They did n't believe in the wise and good,
    Said the best were worst, the wisest fools;
And 't was only to have their teachers taught
    That they founded national schools.

They read in "books that are no books,"
  Their classics — chess-boards neatly bound;
Those their greatest authors who never wrote,
  And their deepest the least profound.

Now, such were the folks of that wonder-land,
  A curious people, as you will own;
But are there none of the race abroad,
  Are no specimens elsewhere known?

Well, I think that he whose views of life
  Are crooked, wrong, perverse, and odd,
Who looks upon all with jaundiced eyes —
  Sees himself and believes it God,

Who sneers at the good, and makes the ill,
  Curses a world he cannot mend;
Who measures life by the rule of wrong
  And abuses its aim and end,

The man who stays when he ought to move,
  And only goes when he ought to stop —
Is strangely like the folk in my dream,
  And would flourish in Turvey Top.

Anonymous.

WHAT THE PRINCE OF I DREAMT

I DREAMT it! such a funny thing —
    And now it's taken wing;
  I s'pose no man before or since
    Dreamt such a funny thing?

It had a Dragon; with a tail;
   A tail both long and slim,
And ev'ry day he wagg'd at it —
   How good it was of him!

And so to him the tailest
   Of all three-tailed Bashaws,
Suggested that for reasons
   The waggling should pause;

And held his tail — which, parting,
   Reversed that Bashaw, which
Reversed that Dragon, who reversed
   Himself into a ditch.

. . . . . .

It had a monkey — in a trap —
   Suspended by the tail:
Oh! but that monkey look'd distress'd,
   And his countenance was pale.

And he had danced and dangled there;
   Till he grew very mad:
For his tail it was a handsome tail
   And the trap had pinched it — bad.

The trapper sat below, and grinn'd;
   His victim's wrath wax'd hot:
He bit his tail in two — and fell —
   And killed him on the spot.

. . . . .

It had a pig — a stately pig;
   With curly tail and quaint:
And the Great Mogul had hold of that
   Till he was like to faint.

So twenty thousand Chinamen,
   With three tails each at least,
Came up to help the Great Mogul,
   And took him round the waist.

And so, the tail slipp'd through his hands;
   And so it came to pass,
That twenty thousand Chinamen
   Sat down upon the grass.

. . . .

It had a Khan — a Tartar Khan —
   With tail superb, I wis;
And that fell graceful down a back
   Which was considered his.

Wherefore all sorts of boys that were
   Accursed, swung by it;
Till he grew savage in his mind
   And vex'd, above a bit:

And so he swept his tail, as one
   Awak'ning from a dream;
And those abominable ones
   Flew off into the stream.

A Nonsense Anthology

Likewise they bobbled up and down,
   Like many apples there;
Till they subsided — and became
   Amongst the things that were.

. . . .

And so it had a moral too,
   That would be bad to lose;
"Whoever takes a Tail in hand
   Should mind his p's and queues."

I dreamt it! — such a funny thing!
   And now it's taken wing;
I s'pose no man before or since
   Dreamt such a funny thing?

                     H. Cholmondeley-Pennell.

THE DINKEY-BIRD *

IN an ocean, 'way out yonder
   (As all sapient people know),
Is the land of Wonder-Wander,
   Whither children love to go;
It's their playing, romping, swinging,
   That give great joy to me
While the Dinkey-Bird goes singing
   In the Amfalula-tree!

There the gum-drops grow like cherries,
   And taffy's thick as peas, —
Caramels you pick like berries
   When, and where, and how you please:

---

* From "Poems of Childhood," copyright, 1892, by Mary French Field; 1894 by Eugene Field.

Big red sugar-plums are clinging
   To the cliffs beside that sea
Where the Dinkey-Bird is singing
   In the Amfalula-tree.

So when children shout and scamper
   And make merry all the day,
When there's naught to put a damper
   To the ardor of their play;
When I hear their laughter ringing,
   Then I'm sure as sure can be
That the Dinkey-Bird is singing
   In the Amfalula-tree.

For the Dinkey-Bird's bravuras
   And staccatos are so sweet —
His roulades, appogiaturas,
   And robustos so complete,
That the youth of every nation —
   Be they near or far away —
Have especial delectation
   In that gladsome roundelay.

Their eyes grow bright and brighter,
   Their lungs begin to crow,
Their hearts get light and lighter,
   And their cheeks are all aglow;
For an echo cometh bringing
   The news to all and me.
That the Dinkey-Bird is singing
   In the Amfalula-tree.

I'm sure you'd like to go there
  To see your feathered friend —
And so many goodies grow there
  You would like to comprehend!
Speed, little dreams, your winging
  To that land across the sea
Where the Dickey-Bird is singing
  In the Amfalula-Tree!

Eugene Field

THE MAN IN THE MOON *

SAID the Raggedy Man on a hot afternoon,
    "My!
        Sakes!
            What a lot o' mistakes
Some little folks makes on the Man in the Moon
But people that's been up to see him like Me,
And calls on him frequent and intimutly,
Might drop a few hints that would interest you
    Clean!
        Through!
            If you wanted 'em to —
Some actual facts that might interest you!

" O the Man in the Moon has a crick in his back
    Whee!
        Whimm!
            Ain't you sorry for him?
And a mole on his nose that is purple and black;

* By permission of the author; from "Rhymes of Childhood,' copyright, 1890, 1898.

And his eyes are so weak that they water and run
If he dares to *dream* even he looks at the sun, —
So he jes' dreams of stars, as the doctors advise —
 My!
  Eyes!
   But is n't he wise —
To jes' dream of stars, as the doctors advise?

"And the Man in the Moon has a boil on his ear —
 Whee!
  Whing!
   What a singular thing!
I know! but these facts are authentic, my dear, —
There 's a boil on his ear; and a corn on his chin,—
He calls it a dimple, — but dimples stick in, —
Yet it might be a dimple turned over, you know!
 Whang!
  Ho!
   Why certainly so! —
It might be a dimple turned over, you know!

"And the Man in the Moon has a rheumatic knee,
 Gee!
  Whizz!
   What a pity that is!
And his toes have worked round where his heels ought to be.
So whenever he wants to go North he goes South,
And comes back with the porridge crumbs all round his mouth,

And he brushes them off with a Japanese fan,
> Whing!
>> Whann!
>>> What a marvellous man!
What a very remarkably marvellous man!

"And the Man in the Moon," sighed the Raggedy Man,
> "Gits!
>> So!
>>> Sullonesome, you know!
Up there by himself since creation began! —
That when I call on him and then come away,
He grabs me and holds me and begs me to stay, —
Till — well, if it was n't for *Jimmy-cum-Jim*,
> Dadd!
>> Limb!
>>> I'd go pardners with him!
Jes' jump my bob here and be pardners with him!"

James Whitcomb Riley.

THE STORY OF THE WILD HUNTSMAN

THIS is the Wild Huntsman that shoots the hares;
With the grass-green coat he always wears;
With game-bag, powder-horn and gun,
He's going out to have some fun.
He finds it hard without a pair
Of spectacles, to shoot the hare.

A Nonsense Anthology

He put his spectacles upon his nose, and said,
"Now I will shoot the hares and kill them dead."
The hare sits snug in leaves and grass,
And laughs to see the green man pass.
Now as the sun grew very hot,
And he a heavy gun had got,
He lay down underneath a tree
And went to sleep as you may see.
And, while he slept like any top,
The little hare came, hop, hop, hop, —
Took gun and spectacles, and then
Softly on tiptoe went off again.
The green man wakes, and sees her place
The spectacles upon her face.
She pointed the gun at the hunter's heart,
Who jumped up at once with a start.
He cries, and screams, and runs away.
"Help me, good people, help! I pray."
At last he stumbled at the well,
Head over ears, and in he fell.
The hare stopped short, took aim, and hark!
Bang went the gun! — she missed her mark!
The poor man's wife was drinking up
Her coffee in her coffee-cup;
The gun shot cup and saucer through;
"Oh dear!" cried she, "what shall I do?"
Hiding close by the cottage there,
Was the hare's own child, the little hare.
When he heard the shot he quickly arose,
And while he stood upon his toes,
The coffee fell and burned his nose;

A Nonsense Anthology

"Oh dear," he cried, "what burns me so?"
And held up the spoon with his little toe.

Dr. Heinrich Hoffman.

THE STORY OF PYRAMID THOTHMES

THOTHMES, who loved a pyramid,
  And dreamed of wonders that it hid,
  Took up again one afternoon,
His longest staff, his sandal shoon,
His evening meal, his pilgrim flask,
And set himself at length the task,
Scorning the smaller and the small,
To climb the highest one of all.

The sun was very hot indeed,
Yet Thothmes never slacked his speed
Until upon the topmost stone
He lightly sat him down alone
To make himself some pleasant cheer
And turned to take his flask of beer,
For he was weary and athirst.
Forth from the neck the stopper burst
And rudely waked the sleeping dead.
In terror guilty Thothmes fled
As rose majestic, wroth and slow,
The Pharaoh's Ka of long ago.
"Help! help!" he cried, "or I am lost!
Oh! save me from old Pharaoh's ghost!"

Till, uttering one fearful yell,
He stumbled at the base and fell
Where Anubis was at his side,
And, by the god of death, he died.

The wife of Thothmes learned his tale
First from the " Memphis Evening Mail,"
And called her son, and told their woe ;
" Alas ! " said she, " I told him so !
Oh, think upon these awful things
And mount not on the graves of kings !
A pyramid is strange to see,
Though only at its base you be."

Anonymous.

THE STORY OF CRUEL PSAMTEK

HERE is cruel Psamtek, see.
  Such a wicked boy was he !
  Chased the ibis round about,
Plucked its longest feathers out,
Stamped upon the sacred scarab
Like an unbelieving Arab,
Put the dog and cat to pain,
Making them to howl again.
Only think what he would do —
Tease the awful Apis too !
Basking by the sacred Nile
Lay the trusting crocodile ;
Cruel Psamtek crept around him,
  Laughed to think how he had found him,

With his pincers seized his tail,
Made the holy one to wail;
Till a priest of Isis came,
Called the wicked boy by name,
Shut him in a pyramid,
Where his punishment was hid.
— But the crocodile the while
Bore the pincers up the Nile —
Here the scribe who taught him letters,
And respect for all his betters,
Gave him many a heavy task,
Horrid medicines from a flask,
While on bread and water, too,
Bitter penance must he do.

The Crocodile is blythe and gay,
With friends and family at play,
And cries, " O blessed Land of Nile,
Where sacred is the crocodile,
Where no ill deed unpunished goes,
And man himself rewards our foes!"

Anonymous.

THE CUMBERBUNCE

I STROLLED beside the shining sea,
I was as lonely as could be;
No one to cheer me in my walk
But stones and sand, which cannot talk —
Sand and stones and bits of shell,
Which never have a thing to tell.

* By permission of Life Publishing Co.; from "Life," copyright.

But as I sauntered by the tide
I saw a something at my side,
A something green, and blue, and pink,
And brown, and purple, too, I think.
I would not say how large it was;
I would not venture that, because
It took me rather by surprise,
And I have not the best of eyes.

Should you compare it to a cat,
I'd say it was as large as that;
Or should you ask me if the thing
Was smaller than a sparrow's wing,
I should be apt to think you knew,
And simply answer, "Very true!"

Well, as I looked upon the thing,
It murmured, "Please, sir, can I sing?"
And then I knew its name at once —
It plainly was a Cumberbunce.

You are amazed that I could tell
The creature's name so quickly? Well,
I knew it was not a paper-doll,
A pencil or a parasol,
A tennis-racket or a cheese,
And, as it was not one of these,
And I am not a perfect dunce —
It had to be a Cumberbunce!

With pleading voice and tearful eye
It seemed as though about to cry.
It looked so pitiful and sad
It made me feel extremely bad.
My heart was softened to the thing
That asked me if it, please, could sing.
Its little hand I longed to shake,
But, oh, it had no hand to take!
I bent and drew the creature near,
And whispered in its pale blue ear,
" What! Sing, my Cumberbunce? You can!
Sing on, sing loudly, little man!"

The Cumberbunce, without ado,
Gazed sadly on the ocean blue,
And, lifting up its little head,
In tones of awful longing, said:

" Oh, I would sing of mackerel skies,
    And why the sea is wet,
Of jelly-fish and conger-eels,
    And things that I forget.
And I would hum a plaintive tune
    Of why the waves are hot
As water boiling on a stove,
    Excepting that they're not!

" And I would sing of hooks and eyes,
    And why the sea is slant,
And gayly tips the little ships,
    Excepting that I can't!

I never sang a single song,
   I never hummed a note.
There is in me no melody,
   No music in my throat.

"So that is why I do not sing
Of sharks, or whales, or anything!"

I looked in innocent surprise,
My wonder showing in my eyes.
"Then why, O, Cumberbunce," I cried,
"Did you come walking at my side
And ask me if you, please, might sing,
When you could not warble anything?"

"I did not ask permission, sir,
I really did not, I aver.
You, sir, misunderstood me, quite.
I did not ask you if I *might*.
Had you correctly understood,
You'd know I asked you if I *could*.
So, as I cannot sing a song,
Your answer, it is plain, was wrong.
The fact I could not sing I knew,
But wanted your opinion, too."

   A voice came softly o'er the lea.
   "Farewell! my mate is calling me!"

I saw the creature disappear,
Its voice, in parting, smote my ear —
"I thought all people understood
The difference 'twixt 'might' and 'could'!"

Paul West.

THE AHKOND OF SWAT

WHO, or why, or which, or *what*,
                Is the Ahkond of Swat?

Is he tall or short, or dark or fair?
Does he sit on a stool or sofa or chair,   or Squat,
               The Ahkond of Swat?

Is he wise or foolish, young or old?
Does he drink his soup and his coffee cold,   or Hot,
               The Ahkond of Swat?

Does he sing or whistle, jabber or talk,
And when riding abroad does he gallop or walk,
                      or Trot,
               The Ahkond of Swat?

Does he wear a turban, a fez or a hat?
Does he sleep on a mattress, a bed or a mat,
                      or a Cot,
               The Ahkond of Swat?

When he writes a copy in round-hand size,
Does he cross his t's and finish his i's
                      with a Dot,
               The Ahkond of Swat?

Can he write a letter concisely clear,
Without a speck or a smudge or smear   or Blot,
               The Ahkond of Swat?

A Nonsense Anthology

Do his people like him extremely well?
Or do they, whenever they can, rebel,   or Plot,
        At the Ahkond of Swat?

If he catches them tnen, either old or young,
Does he have them chopped in pieces or hung,
                    or Shot,
        The Ahkond of Swat?

Do his people prig in the lanes or park?
Or even at times, when days are dark,   Garotte?
        Oh, the Ahkond of Swat?

Does he study the wants of his own dominion?
Or doesn't he care for public opinion   a Jot,
        The Ahkond of Swat?

To amuse his mind do his people show him
Pictures, or any one's last new poem,   or What,
        For the Ahkond of Swat?

At night if he suddenly screams and wakes,
Do they bring him only a few small cakes,
                    or a Lot,
        For the Ahkond of Swat?

Does he live on turnips, tea or tripe,
Does he like his shawl to be marked with a stripe
                    or a Dot,
        The Ahkond of Swat?

Does he like to lie on his back in a boat
Like the lady who lived in that isle remote,
                              Shalott.
                   The Ahkond of Swat?

Is he quiet, or always making a fuss?
Is his steward a Swiss or a Swede or a Russ,
                              or a Scot,
                   The Ahkond of Swat?

Does he like to sit by the calm blue wave?
Or to sleep and snore in a dark green cave,
                              or a Grott,
                   The Ahkond of Swat?

Does he drink small beer from a silver jug?
Or a bowl? or a glass? or a cup? or a mug?
                              or a Pot,
                   The Ahkond of Swat?

Does he beat his wife with a gold-topped pipe,
When she lets the gooseberries grow too ripe,
                              or Rot,
                   The Ahkond of Swat?

Does he wear a white tie when he dines with his friends,
And tie it neat in a bow with ends,   or a Knot,
                   The Ahkond of Swat?

Does he like new cream, and hate mince-pies?
When he looks at the sun does he wink his eyes,
>> or Not,
>> The Ahkond of Swat?

Does he teach his subjects to roast and bake?
Does he sail about on an inland lake,
>> in a Yacht,
>> The Ahkond of Swat?

Some one, or nobody knows I wot
Who or which or why or what
>> Is the Ahkond of Swat!

>> *Edward Lear.*

A THRENODY

WHAT, what, what,
> What's the news from Swat?
> Sad news,
> Bad news,
Comes by the cable led
Through the Indian Ocean's bed,
Through the Persian Gulf, the Red
Sea and the Med-
Iterranean — he's dead;
The Ahkoond is dead!

For the Ahkoond I mourn,
　　Who would n't?
He strove to disregard the mesage stern,
　　But he Ahkood n't.
Dead, dead, dead;
　　(Sorrow Swats!)
Swats wha hae wi' Ahkoond bled,
Swats whom he hath often led
Onward to a gory bed,
　　Or to Victory,
　　　As the case might be,
　　　　Sorrow Swats!
　　Tears shed,
　　　Tears shed like water,
Your great Ahkoond is dead!
　　That Swats the matter!

Mourn, city of Swat!
Your great Ahkoond is not,
But lain 'mid worms to rot.
His mortal part alone, his soul was caught
　(Because he was a good Ahkoond)
　Up to the bosom of Mahound.
Though earthly walls his frame surround
(Forever hallowed be the ground!)
And sceptics mock the lowly mound
And say "He's now of no Ahkoond!"
　　His soul is in the skies —
The azure skies that bend above his loved
　　　Metropolis of Swat.

He sees with larger, other eyes,
Athwart all earthly mysteries —
He knows what's Swat.

Let Swat bury the great Ahkoond
  With a noise of mourning and of lamentation!
Let Swat bury the great Ahkoond
  With the noise of the mourning of the Swattish nation!
    Fallen is at length
    Its tower of strength,
Its sun is dimmed ere it had nooned;
Dead lies the great Ahkoond,
    The great Ahkoond of Swat
    Is not!

George Thomas Lanigan.

DIRGE OF THE MOOLLA OF KOTAL

Rival of the Akhoond of Swat

I

ALAS, unhappy land; ill-fated spot
  Kotal — though where or what
  On earth Kotal is, the bard has forgot;
Further than this indeed he knoweth not —
It borders upon Swat!

II

When sorrows come, they come not single spies,
    But in battal-
Ions: the gloom that lay on Swat now lies
    Upon Kotal,
On sad Kotal, whose people ululate
For their loved Moolla late.
Put away his little turban,
And his narghileh embrowned,
The lord of Kotal — rural urban —
'S gone unto his last Akhoond,
'S gone to meet his rival Swattan,
'S gone, indeed, but not forgotten.

III

His rival, but in what?
Wherein did the deceased Akhoond of Swat
Kotal's lamented Moolla late,
As it were, emulate?
Was it in the tented field
With crash of sword on shield,
While backward meaner champions reeled
And loud the tom-tom pealed?
Did they barter gash for scar
With the Persian scimetar
Or the Afghanistee tulwar,
While loud the tom-tom pealed —
While loud the tom-tom pealed,
And the jim-jam squealed,
And champions less well heeled
Their war-horses wheeled

And fled the presence of these mortal big bugs o'
    the field?
Was Kotal's proud citadel —
Bastioned, and demi-luned,
Beaten down with shot and shell
By the guns of the Akhoond?
Or were wails despairing caught, as
The burghers pale of Swat
Cried in panic, "Moolla ad Portas"?
    — Or what?
Or made each in the cabinet his mark
Kotalese Gortschakoff, Swattish Bismarck?
Did they explain and render hazier
The policies of Central Asia?
Did they with speeches from the throne,
    Wars dynastic,
Ententes cordiales,
Between Swat and Kotal;
Holy alliances,
And other appliances
Of statesmen with morals and consciences
    plastic
Come by much more than their own?
Made they mots, as "There to-day are
No more Himalayehs,"
Or, if you prefer it, "There to-day are
No more Himalaya"?
Or, said the Akhoond, "Sah,
L'État de Swat c'est moi"?
Khabu, did there come great fear
On thy Khabuldozed Ameer
    Ali Shere?

Or did the Khan of far
    Kashgar
Tremble at the menace hot
Of the Moolla of Kotal,
"I will extirpate thee, pal
Of my foe the Akhoond of Swat"?
    Who knows
Of Moolla and Akhoond aught more than I did?
Namely, in life they rivals were, or foes,
And in their deaths not very much divided?
If any one knows it,
Let him disclose it!

George Thomas Lanigan.

RUSSIAN AND TURK

THERE was a Russian came over the sea,
    Just when the war was growing hot;
    And his name it was Tjalikavakaree-
Karindobrolikanahudarot-
    Shibkadirova-
    Ivarditztova
    Sanilik
    Danerik
    Varagobhot.

A Turk was standing upon the shore-
    Right where the terrible Russian crossed,
And he cried: "Bismillah! I'm Ab-El Kor-
Bazarou-Kilgonautosgobross-

> Getfinpravadi-
> Kligekoladji
> Grivino
> Blivido-
> Jenikodosk!

So they stood like brave men long and well;
  And they called each other their proper names,
Till the lockjaw seized them, and where they fell
  They buried them both by the Irdesholmmes
> Kalatalustchuk
> Mischtaribusiclup-
> Bulgari-
> Dulbary-
> Sagharimsing.

Anonymous.

LINES TO MISS FLORENCE HUNTINGDON

SWEET maiden of Passamaquoddy,
  Shall we seek for communion of souls
  Where the deep Mississippi meanders,
Or the distant Saskatchewan rolls?

Ah no, — for in Maine I will find thee
  A sweetly sequestrated nook,
Where the far-winding Skoodoowabskooksis
  Conjoins with the Skoodoowabskook.

There wander two beautiful rivers,
  With many a winding and crook;
The one is the Skoodoowabskooksis,
  The other — the Skoodoowabskook.

Ah, sweetest of haunts! though unmentioned
  In geography, atlas, or book,
How fair is the Skoodoowabskooksis,
  When joining the Skoodoowabskook!

Our cot shall be close by the waters
  Within that sequestrated nook —
Reflected in Skoodoowabskooksis
  And mirrored in Skoodoowabskook.

You shall sleep to the music of leaflets,
  By zephyrs in wantonness shook,
And dream of the Skoodoowabskooksis,
  And, perhaps, of the Skoodoowabskook.

When awaked by the hens and the roosters,
  Each morn, you shall joyously look
On the junction of Skoodoowabskooksis
  With the soft gliding Skoodoowabskook.

Your food shall be fish from the waters,
  Drawn forth on the point of a hook,
From murmuring Skoodoowabskooksis,
  Or wandering Skoodoowabskook!

You shall quaff the most sparkling of water,
   Drawn forth from a silvery brook
Which flows to the Skoodoowabskooksis,
   And then to the Skoodoowabskook!

And you shall preside at the banquet,
   And I will wait on thee as cook;
And we'll talk of the Skoodoowabskooksis,
   And sing of the Skoodoowabskook!

Let others sing loudly of Saco,
   Of Quoddy, and Tattamagouche,
Of Kennebeccasis, and Quaco,
   Of Merigonishe, and Buctouche,

Of Nashwaak, and Magaguadavique,
   Or Memmerimammericook, —
There's none like the Skoodoowabskooksis,
   Excepting the Skoodoowabskook!

Anonymous.

COBBE'S PROPHECIES

WHEN the day and the night do meete
   And the houses are even with the streete:
   And the fire and the water agree,
And blinde men have power to see:
When the Wolf and the Lambe lie down togither,
And the blasted trees will not wither:
When the flood and the ebbe run one way,
And the Sunne and the Moone are at a stay;

When Age and Youth are all one,
And the Miller creepes through the Mill-stone:
When the Ram butts the Butcher on the head,
And the living are buried with the dead.
When the Cobler doth worke without his ends,
And the Cutpurse and the Hangman are friends:
Strange things will then be to see,
But I think it will never be!

— *1614.*

AN UNSUSPECTED FACT

IF down his throat a man should choose
  In fun, to jump or slide,
 He'd scrape his shoes against his teeth,
  Nor dirt his own inside.
But if his teeth were lost and gone,
And not a stump to scrape upon,
He'd see at once how very pat
His tongue lay there by way of mat,
And he would wipe his feet on *that!*

Edward Cannon.

THE SORROWS OF WERTHER

WERTHER had a love for Charlotte
  Such as words could never utter;
   Would you know how first he met her?
 She was cutting bread and butter.

Charlotte was a married lady,
  And a moral man was Werther,
And for all the wealth of Indies,
  Would do nothing for to hurt her.

So he sigh'd and pined and ogled,
  And his passion boil'd and bubbled,
Till he blew his silly brains out,
  And no more was by it troubled.

Charlotte, having seen his body
  Borne before her on a shutter,
Like a well-conducted person,
  Went on cutting bread and butter.

W. M. Thackeray.

NONSENSE VERSES

LAZY-BONES, lazy-bones, wake up and peep!
  The cat's in the cupboard, your mother's asleep.
There you sit snoring, forgetting her ills;
Who is to give her her Bolus and Pills?
Twenty fine Angels must come into town,
All for to help you to make your new gown:
Dainty aerial Spinsters and Singers;
Are n't you ashamed to employ such white fingers?
Delicate hands, unaccustom'd to reels,
To set 'em working a poor body's wheels?
Why they came down is to me all a riddle,
And left Hallelujah broke off in the middle:

Jove's Court, and the Presence angelical, cut —
To eke out the work of a lazy young slut.
Angel-duck, Angel-duck, winged and silly,
Pouring a watering-pot over a lily,
Gardener gratuitous, careless of pelf,
Leave her to water her lily herself,
Or to neglect it to death if she chuse it:
Remember the loss is her own if she lose it.

Charles Lamb.

THE NOBLE TUCK--MAN

AMERICUS, as he did wend
   With A. J. Mortimer, his chum,
The two were greeted by a friend,
"And how are you, boys, Hi, Ho, Hum?"

He spread a note so crisp, so neat
   (Ho, and Hi, and tender Hum),
"If you of this a fifth can eat
   I'll give you the remainder. Come!"

To the tuck-shop three repair,
   (Ho, and Hum, and pensive Hi),
One looks on to see all's fair,
   Two call out for hot mince-pie.

Thirteen tarts, a few Bath buns
   (Hi, and Hum, and gorgeous Ho),
Lobster cakes (the butter'd ones),
   All at once they cry, "No go."

Then doth tuck-man smile. "Them there
  (Ho, and Hi, and futile Hum)
Jellies three and sixpence air,
  Use of spoons an equal sum."

Three are rich. Sweet task 't is o'er,
  "Tuckman, you're a brick," they cry,
Wildly then shake hands all four
  (Hum and Ho, the end is Hi).

Jean Ingelow.

THE PESSIMIST *

NOTHING to do but work,
    Nothing to eat but food,
    Nothing to wear but clothes
To keep one from going nude.

Nothing to breathe but air,
  Quick as a flash 't is gone;
Nowhere to fall but off,
  Nowhere to stand but on.

Nothing to comb but hair,
  Nowhere to sleep but in bed,
Nothing to weep but tears,
  Nothing to bury but dead.

* By permission of Forbes & Co.; from "Ben King's Verses," copyright, 1894, 1898.

Nothing to sing but songs,
    Ah, well, alas! alack!
Nowhere to go but out,
    Nowhere to come but back.

Nothing to see but sights,
    Nothing to quench but thirst,
Nothing to have but what we've got;
    Thus thro' life we are cursed.

Nothing to strike but a gait;
    Everything moves that goes.
Nothing at all but common sense
    Can ever withstand these woes.

Ben King.

THE MODERN HIAWATHA

He killed the noble Mudjokivis.
    Of the skin he made him mittens,
    Made them with the fur side inside,
Made them with the skin side outside.
He, to get the warm side inside,
Put the inside skin side outside;
He, to get the cold side outside,
Put the warm side fur side inside.
That's why he put the fur side inside,
Why he put the skin side outside,
Why he turned them inside outside.

Anonymous.

ON THE ROAD*

SAID Folly to Wisdom,
  "Pray, where are we going?"
Said Wisdom to Folly,
  "There's no way of knowing."

Said Folly to Wisdom,
  "Then what shall we do?"
Said Wisdom to Folly,
  "I thought to ask you."

Tudor Jenks.

UNCLE SIMON AND UNCLE JIM

UNCLE Simon he
  Clum up a tree
  To see what he could see
When presentlee
Uncle Jim
Clum up beside of him
And squatted down by he.

Artemus Ward.

POOR DEAR GRANDPAPA

WHAT is the matter with Grandpapa?
  What can the matter be?
  He's broken his leg in trying to spell
Tommy without a T.

D'Arcy W. Thompson.

---
* By permission of the author.

THE SEA-SERPENT

ALL bones but yours will rattle when I say
    I'm the sea-serpent from America.
    Mayhap you've heard that I've been round the world;
I guess I'm round it now, Mister, twice curled.
Of all the monsters through the deep that splash,
I'm "number one" to all immortal smash.
When I lie down and would my length unroll,
There ar'n't half room enough 'twixt pole and pole.
In short, I grow so long that I've a notion
I must be measured soon for a new ocean.

Planché.

MELANCHOLIA

I AM a peevish student, I;
    My star is gone from yonder sky.
    I think it went so high at first
That it just went and gone and burst.

Anonymous.

THE MONKEY'S WEDDING

THE monkey married the Baboon's sister,
    Smacked his lips and then he kissed her,
    He kissed so hard he raised a blister.
        She set up a yell.

The bridesmaid stuck on some court plaster,
It stuck so fast it could n't stick faster,
Surely 't was a sad disaster,
>   But it soon got well.

What do you think the bride was dressed in?
White gauze veil and a green glass breast-pin,
Red kid shoes — she was quite interesting,
>   She was quite a belle.

The bridegroom swell'd with a blue shirt collar,
Black silk stock that cost a dollar,
Large false whiskers the fashion to follow;
>   He cut a monstrous swell.

What do you think they had for supper?
Black-eyed peas and bread and butter,
Ducks in the duck-house all in a flutter,
>   Pickled oysters too.

Chestnuts raw and boil'd and roasted,
Apples sliced and onions toasted,
Music in the corner posted,
>   Waiting for the cue.

What do you think was the tune they danced to?
"The drunken Sailor" — sometimes "Jim Crow,"
Tails in the way — and some got pinched, too,
>   'Cause they were too long.

What do you think they had for a fiddle?
An old Banjo with a hole in the middle,
A Tambourine made out of a riddle,
>   And that's the end of my song.

Anonymous.

MR. FINNEY'S TURNIP

MR. FINNEY had a turnip
  And it grew and it grew;
  And it grew behind the barn,
And that turnip did no harm.

There it grew and it grew
  Till it could grow no longer;
Then his daughter Lizzie picked it
  And put it in the cellar.

There it lay and it lay
  Till it began to rot;
And his daughter Susie took it
  And put it in the pot.

And they boiled it and boiled it
  As long as they were able,
And then his daughters took it
  And put it on the table.

Mr. Finney and his wife
  They sat down to sup;
And they ate and they ate
  And they ate that turnip up.

Anonymous.

THE SUN

THE Sun, yon glorious orb of day,
　　Ninety-four million miles away,
　　Will keep revolving in its orbit
Till heat and motion reabsorb it.

J. Davis.

THE AUTUMN LEAVES

THE Autumn leaves are falling,
　　Are falling here and there.
　　They're falling through the atmosphere
And also through the air.

Anonymous.

IN THE NIGHT

THE night was growing old
　　As she trudged through snow and sleet;
　　Her nose was long and cold,
And her shoes were full of feet.

Anonymous.

POOR BROTHER

HOW very sad it is to think
　　Our poor benighted brother
　　Should have his head upon one end,
His feet upon the other.

Anonymous.

THE BOY*

DOWN through the snow-drifts in the street
    With blustering joy he steers;
  His rubber boots are full of feet
And his tippet full of ears.

Eugene Field.

THE SEA

BEHOLD the wonders of the mighty deep,
    Where crabs and lobsters learn to creep,
    And little fishes learn to swim,
And clumsy sailors tumble in.

Anonymous.

THERE WAS A LITTLE GIRL

THERE was a little girl,
    And she had a little curl
      Right in the middle of her forehead.
When she was good
She was very, very good,
    And when she was bad she was horrid.

One day she went upstairs,
When her parents, unawares,
    In the kitchen were occupied with meals
And she stood upon her head
In her little trundle-bed,
    And then began hooraying with her heels.

* From "Sharps and Flats," copyright, 1900, by Julia Sutherland Field.

Her mother heard the noise,
And she thought it was the boys
   A-playing at a combat in the attic;
But when she climbed the stair,
And found Jemima there,
   She took and she did spank her most emphatic.

H. W. Longfellow.

FIN DE SIÈCLE

THE sorry world is sighing now;
   La Grippe is at the door;
   And many folks are dying now
Who never died before.

Newton Mackintosh.

MARY JANE

MARY JANE was a farmer's daughter,
   Mary Jane did what she oughter.
   She fell in love — but all in vain;
Oh, poor Mary! oh, poor Jane!

Anonymous.

TENDER–HEARTEDNESS *

LITTLE Willie, in the best of sashes,
   Fell in the fire and was burned to ashes.
   By and by the room grew chilly,
But no one liked to poke up Willie.

Col. D. Streamer.

* By permission of R. H. Russell; from "Ruthless Rhymes for Heartless Homes," copyright, 1901.

IMPETUOUS SAMUEL *

SAM had spirits naught could check,
   And to-day, at breakfast, he
   Broke his baby sister's neck,
So he sha'n't have jam for tea!
Col. D. Streamer.

MISFORTUNES NEVER COME SINGLY *

MAKING toast at the fireside,
   Nurse fell in the grate and died;
   And, what makes it ten times worse,
All the toast was burned with Nurse.
Col. D. Streamer.

AUNT ELIZA *

IN the drinking-well
   (Which the plumber built her)
Aunt Eliza fell, —
We must buy a filter.
Col. D. Streamer.

SUSAN

SUSAN poisoned her grandmother's tea;
   Grandmamma died in agonee.
   Susan's papa was greatly vexed,
And he said to Susan, "My dear, what next?"
Anonymous.

---

* By permission of R. H. Russell; from "Ruthless Rhymes for Heartless Homes," copyright, 1901.

BABY AND MARY

BABY sat on the window-seat;
  Mary pushed Baby into the street;
  Baby's brains were dashed out in the "arey,"
And mother held up her forefinger at Mary.

Anonymous.

THE SUNBEAM

I DINED with a friend in the East, one day,
   Who had no window-sashes;
  A sunbeam through the window came
And burnt his wife to ashes.
"John, sweep your mistress away," said he,
"And bring fresh wine for my friend and me."

Anonymous.

LITTLE WILLIE

LITTLE Willie hung his sister,
  She was dead before we missed her.
  "Willie's always up to tricks!
Ain't he cute? He's only six!"

Anonymous.

MARY AMES

PITY now poor Mary Ames,
  Blinded by her brother James;
  Red-hot nails in her eyes he poked, —
I never saw Mary more provoked.

Anonymous.

MUDDLED METAPHORS

By a Moore-ose Melodist

OH, ever thus from childhood's hour,
  I've seen my fondest hopes recede!
  I never loved a tree or flower
That did n't trump its partner's lead.

I never nursed a dear gazelle,
  To glad me with its dappled hide,
But when it came to know me well,
  It fell upon the buttered side.

I never taught a cockatoo
  To whistle comic songs profound,
But, just when "Jolly Dogs" it knew,
  It failed for ninepence in the pound.

I never reared a walrus cub
  In my aquarium to plunge,
But, when it learned to love its tub,
  It placidly threw up the sponge!

I never strove a metaphor
  To every bosom home to bring
But — just as it had reached the door —
  It went and cut a pigeon's wing!

Tom Hood, Jr.

VILLON'S STRAIGHT TIP TO ALL CROSS COVES

"Tout aux tavernes et aux fiells"

SUPPOSE you screeve? or go cheap-jack?
  Or fake the broads? or fig a nag?
  Or thimble-rig? or knap a yack?
  Or pitch a snide? or smash a rag?
  Suppose you duff? or nose and lag?
Or get the straight, and land your pot?
  How do you melt the multy swag?
Booze and the blowens cop the lot.

Fiddle, or fence, or mace, or mack;
  Or moskeneer, or flash the drag;
Dead-lurk a crib, or do a crack;
  Pad with a slang, or chuck a fag;
  Bonnet, or tout, or mump and gag;
Rattle the tats, or mark the spot;
  You cannot bag a single stag;
Booze and the blowens cop the lot.

Suppose you try a different tack,
    And on the square you flash your flag?
At penny-a-lining make your whack,
    Or with the mummers mug and gag?
    For nix, for nix the dibbs you bag!
At any graft, no matter what,
    Your merry goblins soon stravag:
Booze and the blowens cop the lot.

The Moral

It's up the spout and Charley Wag
With wipes and tickers and what not
    Until the squeezer nips your scrag,
Booze and the blowens cop the lot.

W. E. Henley.

ODE TO THE HUMAN HEART

BLIND Thamyris, and blind Mæonides,
    Pursue the triumph and partake the gale!
    Drop tears as fast as the Arabian trees,
To point a moral or adorn a tale.

Full many a gem of purest ray serene,
    Thoughts that do often lie too deep for tears,
Like angels' visits, few and far between,
    Deck the long vista of departed years.

Man never is, but always to be bless'd;
  The tenth transmitter of a foolish face,
Like Aaron's serpent, swallows up the rest,
  And makes a sunshine in the shady place.

For man the hermit sigh'd, till woman smiled,
  To waft a feather or to drown a fly,
(In wit a man, simplicity a child,)
  With silent finger pointing to the sky.

But fools rush in where angels fear to tread,
  Far out amid the melancholy main;
As when a vulture on Imaus bred,
  Dies of a rose in aromatic pain.

Laman Blanchard.

LIMERICKS

THERE was an old person of Ware
Who rode on the back of a bear;
   When they said, "Does it trot?"
   He said: "Certainly not,
It's a Moppsikon Floppsikon bear."

THERE was an old person of Wick,
Who said, "Tick-a-Tick, Tick-a-Tick,
   Chickabee, Chickabaw,"
   And he said nothing more,
This laconic old person of Wick.

THERE was an old person of Woking,
Whose mind was perverse and provoking;
   He sate on a rail,
   With his head in a pail,
That illusive old person of Woking.

THERE was once a man with a beard
Who said, "It is just as I feared! —
   Two Owls and a Hen,
   Four Larks and a Wren
Have all built their nests in my beard."

THERE was an old man of Thermopylæ,
Who never did anything properly;
    But they said: "If you choose
    To boil eggs in your shoes,
You cannot remain in Thermopylæ."

THERE was an Old Man who said, "Hush!
I perceive a young bird in this bush!"
    When they said, "Is it small?"
    He replied, "Not at all;
It is four times as big as the bush!"

THERE was an Old Man who supposed
That the street door was partially closed;
    But some very large Rats
    Ate his coats and his hats,
While that futile Old Gentleman dozed.

THERE was an Old Man of Leghorn,
The smallest that ever was born;
    But quickly snapt up he
    Was once by a Puppy,
Who devoured that Old Man of Leghorn.

THERE was an Old Man of Kamschatka
Who possessed a remarkably fat Cur;
    His gait and his waddle
    Were held as a model
To all the fat dogs in Kamschatka.

                    Edward Lear.

[*From books printed for the benefit of the New York Fair in aid of the Sanitary Commission,* 1864]

There was a gay damsel of Lynn,
  Whose waist was so charmingly thin,
    The dressmaker needed
    A microscope — she did —
To fit this slim person of Lynn.

There was a young lady of Milton,
Who was highly disgusted with Stilton;
    When offered a bite,
    She said, "Not a mite!"
That suggestive young lady of Milton.

There was a dear lady of Eden,
Who on apples was quite fond of feedin';
    She gave one to Adam,
    Who said, "Thank you, Madam,"
And then both skedaddled from Eden.

There was a young lady of Wales,
Who wore her back hair in two tails;
    And a hat on her head
    That was striped black and red,
And studded with ten-penny nails.

A Nonsense Anthology

There was an old man who said, "Do
Tell me how I'm to add two and two?
   I'm not very sure
   That it does n't make four —
But I fear that is almost too few."

There once was a man who said, "How
Shall I manage to carry my cow?
   For if I should ask it
   To get in my basket,
'T would make such a terrible row."

Anonymous.

There once was an old man of Lyme
   Who married three wives at a time;
     When asked, "Why a third?"
     He replied, "One's absurd!
And bigamy, sir, is a crime."

There once was a person of Benin,
Who wore clothes not fit to be seen in;
   When told that he should n't,
   He replied, "Gumscrumrudent!"
A word of inscrutable meanin'.

THERE once was a girl of New York
Whose body was lighter than cork;
   She had to be fed
   For six weeks upon lead,
Before she went out for a walk.

Cosmo Monkhouse.

THERE was a young man who was bitten
  By twenty-two cats and a kitten;
   Sighed he, "It is clear
   My finish is near;
No matter; I'll die like a Briton!"

THERE was a princess of Bengal,
Whose mouth was exceedingly small;
   Said she, "It would be
   More easy for me
To do without eating at all!"

THERE was an old stupid who wrote
The verses above that we quote;
   His want of all sense
   Was something immense,
Which made him a person of note.

Walter Parke.

VERS NONSENSIQUES

À POTSDAM, les totaux absteneurs,
    Comme tant d'autres titotalleurs,
        Sont gloutons, omnivores,
        Nasorubicolores,
Grands manchons, et terribles duffeurs.

Un vieux duc (le meilleur des époux)
Demandait (en lui tâtant le pouls)
    À sa vielle duchesse
    (Qu'un vieux catarrhe oppresse) : —
" Et ton thé, t'a-t-il ôté ta toux ? "

Il naquit près de Choisy-le-Roi ;
Le Latin lui causait de l'effroi ;
    Et les Mathématiques
    Lui donnaient des coliques,
Et le Grec l'enrhûmait. Ce fut moi.

Il était un gendarme, à Nanteuil,
Qui n'avait qu'une dent et qu'un œil ;
    Mais cet œil solitaire
    Etait plein de mystère ;
Cette dent, d'importance et d'orgueil.

" Cassez-vous, cassez-vous, cassez-vous,
O mer, sur vos froids gris calloux ! "
    Ainsi traduisit Laure
    Au profit d'Isadore
(Bon jeune homme, at son futur epoux.)

Un marin naufragé (de Doncastre)
Pour prière, au milieu du désastre
    Répétait à genoux
    Ces mots simples et doux : —
"Scintillez, scintillez, petit astre!"

George du Maurier.

THERE was a young man of Cohoes,*
  Wore tar on the end of his nose;
    When asked why he done it,
    He said for the fun it
Afforded the men of Cohoes.

Robert J. Burdette.

I'D rather have habits than clothes,
  For that's where my intellect shows.
    And as for my hair,
    Do you think I should care
To comb it at night with my toes?

I WISH that my Room had a Floor;
I don't so much care for a Door,
    But this walking around
    Without touching the ground
Is getting to be quite a bore!

Gelett Burgess.

* By permission of the author.

A Nonsense Anthology

'TWAS an indigent Hen,
　Who picked up a corn now and then;
　　She had but one leg
　　On which she could peg,
And behind her left ear was a wen.

Bruce Porter.

CLEOPATRA, who thought they maligned her,
　Resolved to reform and be kinder;
　　"If, when pettish," she said,
　　"I should knock off your head,
Won't you give me some gentle reminder?"

Newton Mackintosh.

WHEN that Seint George hadde sleyne ye draggon,
　He sate him down furninst a flaggon;
　　And, wit ye well,
　　Within a spell
He had a bien plaisaunt jag on.

Anonymous.

THERE was a young lady of Niger
    Who smiled as she rode on a Tiger;
    They came back from the ride
    With the lady inside,
And the smile on the face of the Tiger.

Anonymous.

THERE was a young maid who said, "Why
    Can't I look in my ear with my eye?
    If I give my mind to it,
    I'm sure I can do it,
You never can tell till you try."

INDEX OF TITLES

INDEX OF TITLES

ABSTEMIA	*Gelett Burgess*	38
Abstrosophy	*Gelett Burgess*	37
Æstivation	*O. W. Holmes*	136
Ahkond of Swat, The	*Edward Lear*	230
Alone		40
As with my Hat upon my Head	*Dr. Johnson*	xxx
Auld Wife, The	*C. S. Calverley*	192
Aunt Eliza	*Col. D. Streamer*	254
Autumn Leaves, The		251
BABY AND MARY		255
Ballade of the Nurserie	*John Twig*	60
Ballad of Bedlam		24
Ballad of High Endeavor, A		62
Ballad with an Ancient Refrain		65
Bison, The	*Hilaire Belloc*	209
Bloated Biggaboon, The	*H. Cholmondeley-Pennell*	211
Blue Moonshine	*Francis G. Stokes*	46
Boy, The	*Eugene Field*	252
Bulbul, The	*Owen Seaman*	65
Buz, quoth the Blue Fly	*Ben Jonson*	66
CENTIPEDE, A		xxxi
Chimpanzee, The	*Oliver Herford*	199
Chronicle, A		155
Classic Ode, A	*Charles Battell Loomis*	45
Cobbe's Prophecies		241
Cock and the Bull, The	*C. S. Calverley*	165
Collusion between a Alegaiter and a Water-Snaik	*J. W. Morris*	143
Companions	*C. S. Calverley*	163

[271]

Cossimbazar	Henry S. Leigh	43
Cow, The	Oliver Herford	198
Cruise of the "P. C.", The		13
Cumberbunce, The	Paul West	226
DARWINITY	Herman Merivale	31
Dinkey-Bird, The	Eugene Field	218
Dirge of the Moolla of Kotal	George T. Lanigan	235
ELDERLY GENTLEMAN, THE	George Canning	134
Elegy on the Death of a Mad Dog	Oliver Goldsmith	151
Elegy on Madam Blaize	Oliver Goldsmith	149
FAITHLESS NELLY GRAY	Thomas Hood	131
Famous Ballad of the Jubilee Cup, The	A. T. Quiller-Couch	175
Father William		22
Ferdinando and Elvira	W. S. Gilbert	160
Fin de Siècle	Newton Mackintosh	253
Flamingo, The	Lewis Gaylord Clark	201
Forcing a Way		54
Frangipanni		51
Frog, The	Hilaire Belloc	207
GENERAL JOHN	W. S. Gilbert	112
Gentle Alice Brown	W. S. Gilbert	102
Great Man, A	Oliver Goldsmith	148
Guinea Pig, The		68
HEN, THE	Oliver Herford	197
Her Dairy	Peter Newell	213
Here is the Tale	Anthony C. Deane	188
Her Polka Dots	Peter Newell	212
Higher Pantheism in a Nutshell, The	A. C. Swinburne	30
Hippopotamus, The	Oliver Herford	199
Holiday Task, A	Gilbert Abbott à Becket	137
Hunting of the Snark, The	Lewis Carroll	97

Index of Titles

Hyder iddle diddle dell		73
Hymn to the Sunrise		25
IF		70
If Half the Road		xxxiii
If a Man who Turnips Cries	Dr. Johnson	xxxi
I Love to Stand		xxxiii
Imitation of Wordsworth	Catharine M. Fanshawe	173
Impetuous Samuel	Col. D. Streamer	254
Incidents in the Life of my Uncle Arly	Edward Lear	86
Indifference		42
In Immemorian	Cuthbert Bede	29
In the Dumps		74
In the Gloaming	James C. Bayles	23
In the Night		251
Invisible Bridge, The	Gelett Burgess	196
JABBERWOCKY	Lewis Carroll	3
John Jones	A. C. Swinburne	57
Jumblies, The	Edward Lear	83
KEN YE AUGHT O' CAPTAIN GROSE	Robert Burns	xxiv
Kindness to Animals	J. Ashby-Sterry	203
King Arthur		73
LAYE OF YE WOODPECKORE, YE	Henry A. Beers	139
Lazy Roof, The	Gelett Burgess	197
Like to the Thundering Tone	Bishop Corbet	27
LIMERICKS:		
Cleopatra, who thought they maligned her	Newton Mackintosh	267
H was an indigent Hen	Bruce Porter	267
I'd rather have habits than clothes	Gelett Burgess	266
I wish that my room had a floor	Gelett Burgess	266
There once was a girl of New York	Cosmo Monkhouse	264

[273]

LIMERICKS — *Continued*

There once was a man who said "How"		263
There once was an old man of Lyme	*Cosmo Monkhouse*	263
There once was a person of Benin	*Cosmo Monkhouse*	263
There was a dear lady of Eden		262
There was a gay damsel of Lynn		262
There was an old man in a tree	*Edward Lear*	xxx
There was an Old Man of Kamschatka	*Edward Lear*	261
There was an Old Man of Leghorn	*Edward Lear*	261
There was an old man of St. Bees	*W. S. Gilbert*	xxx
There was an old man of Thermopylæ	*Edward Lear*	261
There was an old man who said "Do"		263
There was an Old Man who said "Hush"	*Edward Lear*	261
There was an Old Man who supposed	*Edward Lear*	261
There was an old person of Ware	*Edward Lear*	260
There was an old person of Wick	*Edward Lear*	260
There was an old person of Woking	*Edward Lear*	260
There was an old stupid who wrote	*Walter Parke*	264
There was once a man with a beard	*Edward Lear*	260
There was a princess of Bengal	*Walter Parke*	264

Index of Titles

LIMERICKS — *Continued*

There was a small boy of Quebec	*Rudyard Kipling*	xxxii
There was a young lady of Milton		262
There was a young lady of Niger		268
There was a young lady of Wales		262
There was a young maid who said "Why"		268
There was a young man at St. Kitts		xxv
There was a young man of Cohoes	*Robert J. Burdette*	266
There was a young man who was bitten	*Walter Parke*	264
Vers Nonsensiques	*George du Maurier*	265
When that Seint George hadde sleyne ye draggon		267
Lines by a Fond Lover		53
Lines by a Medium		41
Lines by a Person of Quality	*Alexander Pope*	50
Lines to Miss Florence Huntingdon		239
Lines to a Young Lady	*Edward Lear*	88
Little Billee	*W. M. Thackeray*	114
Little Peach, The		138
Little Willie		255
Lobster wooed a Lady Crab, A		xxxxiii
Lovers and a Reflection	*C. S. Calverley*	170
Love Song by a Lunatic		55
Lugubrious Whing-Whang, The	*James W. Riley*	63
Lunar Stanzas	*H. C. Knight*	15
MALUM OPUS	*J. Appleton Morgan*	135
Man in the Moon, The	*James W. Riley*	220
Martin Luther at Potsdam	*Barry Pain*	160

[275]

Martin to his Man		74
Mary Ames		256
Mary Jane		253
Master and Man		72
Mayor of Scuttleton, The	*Mary Mapes Dodge*	195
Melancholia		248
Metaphysics	*Oliver Herford*	36
Minnie and Winnie	*Lord Tennyson*	194
Misfortunes	*Col. D. Streamer*	254
Mr. Finney's Turnip		250
Modern Hiawatha, The		246
Monkey's Glue, The	*Goldwin Goldsmith*	210
Monkey's Wedding The		248
Monsieur McGinté		139
Moon is up, The		26
Moorlands of the Not		36
Mors Iabrochii		4
Muddled Metaphors	*Tom Hood, Jr.*	256
My Dream		28
My Feet	*Gelett Burgess*	197
My Home		29
My Recollectest Thoughts	*Charles E. Carryl*	21
NEPHELIDIA	*A. C. Swinburne*	158
Noble Tuckman, The	*Jean Ingelow*	244
Nonsense		16
Nonsense	*Thomas Moore*	47
Nonsense Verses	*Charles Lamb*	242
Not I	*R. L. Stevenson*	194
Nyum-Nyum, The		6
OCEAN WANDERER, THE		18
Odd to a Krokis		146
Ode to the Human Heart	*Laman Blanchard*	258
Of Baiting the Lion	*Owen Seaman*	206
Oh, my Geraldine	*F. C. Burnand*	66
Oh, Weary Mother	*Barry Pain*	64
On the Oxford Carrier	*John Milton*	157
On the Road	*Tudor Jenks*	247
Owl and the Pussy-Cat, The	*Edward Lear*	59

Index of Titles

Panther, The		209
Parson Gray	Oliver Goldsmith	150
Parterre, The	E. H. Palmer	56
Personified Sentimental, The	Bret Harte	44
Pessimist, The	Ben King	245
Platypus, The	Oliver Herford	199
Pobble who has no Toes, The	Edward Lear	81
Poor Brother		251
Poor Dear Grandpapa	D'Arcy W. Thompson	247
Psycholophon	Gelett Burgess	39
Puer ex Jersey		138
Purple Cow, The	Gelett Burgess	196
Python, The	Hilaire Belloc	208
Quatrain		43
Riddle, A		70
Rollicking Mastodon, The	Arthur Macy	125
Russian and Turk		238
Sage Counsel	A. T. Quiller-Couch	204
Sailor's Yarn, A	James Jeffrey Roche	120
Sea, The		252
Sea-Serpent, The	Planché	248
She's All my Fancy Painted Him	Lewis Carroll	20
She Went into the Garden	S. Foote	xxxi
Shipwreck, The	E. H. Palmer	118
Silver Question, The	Oliver Herford	127
Sing for the Garish Eye	W. S. Gilbert	13
Singular Sangfroid of Baby Bunting, The	Guy W. Carryl	129
Some Geese	Oliver Herford	200
Some Verses to Snaix		147
Song of Impossibilities	William M. Praed	183
Song of the Screw, The		33
Song on King William III.		67
Sonnet Found in a Deserted Madhouse		18
Sorrows of Werther, The	W. M. Thackeray	242

A Nonsense Anthology

Spirk Troll-Derisive	*James W. Riley*	10
Story of Cruel Psamtek, The		225
Story of Prince Agib, The	*W. S. Gilbert*	107
Story of Pyramid Thothmes		224
Story of the Wild Huntsman	*Heinrich Hoffmann*	222
Sun, The	*J. Davis*	251
Sunbeam, The		255
Superior Nonsense Verses		47
Susan		254
Swiss Air	*Bret Harte*	64
Sylvie and Bruno	*Lewis Carroll*	101
TENDER-HEARTEDNESS	*Col. D. Streamer*	253
Tender Infant, The	*Dr. Johnson*	xxx
There was a Frog		211
There was a Little Girl	*H. W. Longfellow*	252
There was a Monkey		67
Three Acres of Land		71
Three Children		69
Three Jovial Huntsmen		70
Threnody	*George T. Lanigan*	233
Thy Heart		55
Timid Hortense	*Peter Newell*	212
Timon of Archimedes	*Charles Battell Loomis*	39
'T is Midnight and the Setting Sun		26
'T is Sweet to Roam		23
To Marie		14
To Mollidusta	*Planché*	57
Transcendentalism		41
Trust in Women		186
Turvey Top		43
Tweedle-dum and Tweedle-dee		74
UFFIA	*Harriet R. White*	10
Uncle Simon and Uncle Jim	*Artemus Ward*	247
Unsuspected Fact, An	*Edward Cannon*	242
Uprising See the Fitful Lark		27
VILLON'S STRAIGHT TIP	*W. E. Henley*	257

Index of Titles

WALLOPING WINDOW-BLIND, THE	Charles E. Carryl	123
Walrus and the Carpenter, The	Lewis Carroll	93
Ways and Means	Lewis Carroll	90
Whango Tree, The		12
What the Prince of I Dreamt	H. Cholmondeley-Pennell	215
When Moonlike ore the Hazure Seas	W. M. Thackeray	49
Where Avalanches Wail		45
Wild Flowers	Peter Newell	212
Wonderful Old Man, The		153
Wreck of the "Julie Plante"	W. H. Drummond	116
YAK, THE	Hilaire Belloc	111
Yonghy-Bonghy-Bò, The	Edward Lear	76

INDEX OF AUTHORS

INDEX OF AUTHORS

À BECKET, GILBERT ABBOTT
    A Holiday Task 137
ASHBY-STERRY, J.
    Kindness to Animals 203

BAYLES, JAMES C.
    In the Gloaming 23
BEDE, CUTHBERT
    In Immemoriam 29
BEERS, HENRY A.
    Ye Laye of ye Woodpeckore 139
BELLOC, HILAIRE
    The Bison 209
    The Frog 207
    The Python 208
    The Yak 207
BLANCHARD, LAMAN
    Ode to the Human Heart 258
BURDETTE, ROBERT J.
    Limerick 266
BURGESS, GELETT
    Abstemia 38
    Abstrosophy 37
    The Invisible Bridge 196
    The Lazy Roof 197
    Limericks 266
    My Feet 197
    Psycholophon 39
    The Purple Cow 196
BURNAND, F. C.
    Oh, my Geraldine 66

BURNS, ROBERT
    Ken ye Aught o' Captain Grose? 73

CALVERLEY, CHARLES S.
    The Auld Wife 192
    The Cock and the Bull 165
    Companions 163
    Lovers and a Reflection 170

CANNING, GEORGE
    The Elderly Gentleman 134

CANNON, EDWARD
    An Unsuspected Fact 242

CARROLL, LEWIS
    The Hunting of the Snark 97
    Jabberwocky 3
    She's All my Fancy Painted Him 20
    Sylvie and Bruno 101
    The Walrus and the Carpenter 93
    Ways and Means 90

CARRYL, CHARLES E.
    My Recollectest Thoughts 21
    The Walloping Window-Blind 123

CARRYL, GUY WETMORE
    The Singular Sangfroid of Baby Bunting . . . 129

CHOLMONDELEY-PENNELL, H.
    The Bloated Biggaboon 211
    What the Prince of I Dreamt 215

CLARK, LEWIS GAYLORD
    The Flamingo 201

CORBET, BISHOP
    Like to the Thundering Tone 27

DAVIS, J.
    The Sun 251

DEANE, ANTHONY C.
    Here is the Tale 188

DODGE, MARY MAPES
    The Mayor of Scuttleton 195

Index of Authors

DRUMMOND, W. H.
    Wreck of the "Julie Plante," The 116
DU MAURIER, GEORGE
    Vers Nonsensiques 265

FANSHAWE, CATHARINE M.
    Imitation of Wordsworth 173
FIELD, EUGENE
    The Boy 252
    The Dinkey Bird 218
FOOTE, S.
    Farrago of Nonsense xxxi

GILBERT, W. S.
    Ferdinando and Elvira 110
    General John 112
    Gentle Alice Brown 102
    Sing for the Garish Eye 13
    The Story of Prince Agib 107
    There was an Old Man of St. Bees xxx
GOLDSMITH, GOLDWIN
    The Monkey's Glue 210
GOLDSMITH, OLIVER
    Elegy on the Death of a Mad Dog 151
    Elegy on Madam Blaize 149
    A Great Man 148
    Parson Gray 150

HARTE, BRET
    The Personified Sentimental 44
    Swiss Air 64
HENLEY, W. E.
    Villon's Straight Tip 257
HERFORD, OLIVER
    The Chimpanzee 199
    The Cow 198
    The Hen 197
    The Hippopotamus 199
    Metaphysics 36

HERFORD, OLIVER — *Continued*
    The Platypus 199
    The Silver Question 127
    Some Geese 200
HOFFMAN, HEINRICH
    The Story of the Wild Huntsman 222
HOLMES, OLIVER WENDELL
    Æstivation 136
HOOD, THOMAS
    Faithless Nelly Gray 131
HOOD, THOMAS, JR.
    Muddled Metaphors 256

INGELOW, JEAN
    The Noble Tuckman 244

JENKS, TUDOR
    On the Road 247
JOHNSON, SAMUEL
    As with my Hat xxx
    If a Man who Turnips Cries xxxi
    The Tender Infant xxx
JONSON, BEN
    Buz, quoth the Blue Fly 66

KING, BEN
    The Pessimist 245
KIPLING, RUDYARD
    Limerick xxxii
KNIGHT, HENRY C.
    Lunar Stanzas 15

LAMB, CHARLES
    Nonsense Verses 243
LANIGAN, GEORGE T.
    Dirge of the Moolla of Kotal 235
    A Threnody 233
LEAR, EDWARD
    The Ahkond of Swat 230
    Incidents in the Life of my Uncle Arly . . . 86

Index of Authors

LEAR, EDWARD — *Continued*
    The Jumblies 83
    Limericks 260–263
    Lines to a Young Lady 88
    The Owl and the Pussy-Cat 59
    The Pobble 81
    There was an Old Man in a Tree xxx
    The Yonghy-Bonghy-Bo 76

LEIGH, HENRY S.
    Cossimbazar 43

LONGFELLOW, H. W.
    There was a Little Girl 252

LOOMIS, CHARLES BATTELL
    A Classic Ode 45
    Timon of Archimedes 39

MACKINTOSH, NEWTON
    Fin de Siècle 253
    Limerick 267

MACY, ARTHUR
    The Rollicking Mastodon 125

MERIVALE, HERMAN
    Darwinity 31

MILTON, JOHN
    On the Oxford Carrier 157

MONKHOUSE, COSMO
    Limericks 263–264

MOORE, THOMAS
    Nonsense 47

MORGAN, JAMES APPLETON
    Malum Opus 135

MORRIS, J W.
    Collusion between a Alegaiter and a Water-Snaik 143

NEWELL, PETER
    Her Dairy 213
    Her Polka Dots 212
    Timid Hortense 212
    Wild Flowers 212

PAIN, BARRY
    Martin Luther at Potsdam 160
    Oh, Weary Mother 64
PALMER, E. H.
    The Parterre 56
    The Shipwreck 118
PARKE, WALTER
    Limericks 264
PLANCHÉ
    The Sea-Serpent 248
    To Mollidusta 57
POPE, ALEXANDER
    Lines by a Person of Quality 50
PORTER, BRUCE
    Limerick 267
PRAED, W. M.
    Song of Impossibilities 183

QUILLER-COUCH, A. T.
    The Famous Ballad of the Jubilee Cup . . . 175
    Sage Counsel 204

RILEY, JAMES W.
    The Lugubrious Whing-Whang 63
    The Man in the Moon 220
    Spirk Troll-Derisive 10
ROCHE, JAMES JEFFREY
    A Sailor's Yarn 120

SEAMAN, OWEN
    The Bulbul 65
    Of Baiting the Lion 205
STEVENSON, R. L.
    Not I 194
STOKES, FRANCIS G.
    Blue Moonshine 46
STREAMER, COL. D.
    Aunt Eliza 254
    Impetuous Samuel 254

Index of Authors

STREAMER, COL. D. — *Continued*
    Misfortunes 254
    Tender-Heartedness 253
SWINBURNE, A. C.
    The Higher Pantheism 30
    John Jones 57
    Nephelidia 158

TENNYSON, LORD
    Minnie and Winnie 194
THACKERAY, W. M.
    Little Billee 114
    The Sorrows of Werther 242
    When Moonlike ore the Hazure Seas . . . 49
THOMPSON, D'ARCY W.
    Poor Dear Grandpapa 247
TWIG, JOHN
    Ballade of the Nurserie 60

WARD, ARTEMUS
    Uncle Simon and Uncle Jim 247
WEST, PAUL
    The Cumberbur 226
WHITE, HARRIET F.
    Uffia 10

INDEX OF FIRST LINES

A Potsdam, les totaux absteneurs,	265
Across the moorlands of the Not	36
Across the swiffling waves they went,	13
Affection's charm no longer gilds	44
Ah Night! blind germ of days to be,	62
Alas! my Child, where is the Pen	197
Alas, unhappy land; ill-fated spot	235
Alone! Alone!	40
All bones but yours will rattle when I say	248
Americus, as he did wend	244
As a friend to the children commend me the yak,	207
As I walked by myself,	67
As one who cleaves the circumambient air	39
Auld wife sat at her ivied door, The	192
Autumn leaves are falling, The	251
Baby sat on the window-seat;	255
Bartholomew Benjamin Bunting	129
Be kind and tender to the Frog,	207
Be kind to the panther! for when thou wert young,	209
Behold the wonders of the mighty deep,	252
Ben Battle was a soldier bold,	131
Bison is vain, and (I write it with pain), The	209
Blind Thamyris, and blind Maeonides,	258
Bloated Biggaboon, The	211
Bravest names for fire and flames, The	112
Bright breaks the warrior o'er the ocean wave	18
Bulbul hummeth like a book, The	65
Buz, quoth the blue fly,	66
By the side of a murmuring stream an elderly gentleman sat	134

[291]

Index of First Lines

Capital ship for an ocean trip, A	123
"Cassez-vous, cassez-vous, cassez-vous, ...	265
Children, behold the Chimpanzee:	199
Cleopatra, who thought they maligned her, ...	267
Coesper erat: tunc lubriciles ultravia circum	4
Come fleetly, come fleetly, my hookabadar, ...	43
Cow is too well known, I fear, The	198
Crankadox leaned o'er the edge of the moon, The ...	10
Down through the snow-drifts in the street	252
Dreamy crags with raucous voices croon, The	25
Ev-er-y child who has the use	200
Fluttering spread thy purple pinions, ...	50
From the depth of the dreamy decline of the dawn through a notable nimbus of nebulous noonshine,	158
Good people all, of every sort, ...	151
Good people all, with one accord, ...	149
Good reader, if you e'er have seen, ...	47
H was an indigent Hen, ...	267
He comes with herald clouds of dust;	47
He killed the noble Mudjokivis.	246
He thought he saw a Banker's clerk	101
Here is cruel Psamtek, see.	225
Here lieth one, who did most truly prove	157
How many strive to force a way	54
"How pleasant to know Mr. Lear!"	88
How very sad it is to think	251
Hyder iddle diddle dell, ...	73
I am a peevish student, I;	248
I dined with a friend in the East, one day, ...	255
I don't know any greatest treat	56

[292]

Index of First Lines

I dreamed a dream next Tuesday week,	28
I dreamt it! such a funny thing —	215
I know not of what we ponder'd	163
I might not, if I could;	41
I never saw a Purple Cow,	196
I strolled beside the shining sea,	226
I wish that my Room had a Floor;	266
I'd never Dare to Walk across	196
I'd rather have habits than clothes,	266
If all the land were apple-pie,	70
If aught that stumbles in my speech	38
If down his throat a man should choose	242
If echoes from the fitful past	37
Il était un gendarme, à Nanteuil,	265
Il naquit près de Choisy-le-Roi;	265
I'll tell thee everything I can;	90
I'm a gay tra, la, la,	64
In an ocean, 'way out yonder	218
In candent ire the solar splendor flames;	136
In loopy links the canker crawls,	42
In moss-prankt dells which the sunbeams flatter	170
In the drinking-well	254
It is told, in Buddhi-theosophic schools,	41
It is pilly-po-doddle and aligobung	15
It was a robber's daughter, and her name was Alice Brown.	102
Lady, I loved you all last year,	183
Lazy-bones, lazy-bones, wake up and peep!	243
Like to the thundering tone of unspoke speeches,	27
Lilies lie in my lady's bower, The	64
Lion is the beast to fight, The	204
Little Willie hung his sister,	255
Little Willie, in the best of sashes,	253

Index of First Lines

Love me and leave me; what love bids retrieve me? can June's fist grasp May?	57
"Love you?" said I, then I sighed, and then I gazed upon her sweetly —	110
Lovely maid, with rapture swelling,	53
Making toast at the fireside,	254
Man in the winderness asked of me, The	70
Martin said to his man,	74
Mary Jane was a farmer's daughter,	253
Master I have, and I am his man,	72
Mayor of Scuttleton burned his nose, The	195
Milkweed, and a buttercup, and cowslip," said sweet Mary, "A	213
Mingled aye with fragrant yearnings,	46
Minnie and Winnie	194
Mr. Finney had a turnip	250
Monkey married the Baboon's sister, The	248
Monsieur McGinté allait en bas jusqu'au fond du mer,	139
Moon is up, the moon is up!, The	26
Moving form or rigid mass, A	33
My child, the Duck-billed Platypus	199
My father left me three acres of land,	71
My feet, they haul me Round the House,	197
My home is on the rolling deep,	29
My recollectest thoughts are those	21
Night saw the crew like pedlers with their packs	15
Night was growing old, The	251
Nothing to do but work,	245
"Now, if the fish will only bite, we'll have some royal fun."	212
Now Jack looked up — it was time to sup, and the bucket was yet to fill,	188

Index of First Lines

Nyum-Nyum chortled by the sea, The	6
O stoodent A has gone and spent,	65
O whither goest thou, pale studént	139
"Of what are you afraid, my child?" inquired the kindly teacher.	212
Oh, ever thus from childhood's hour,	256
Oh, lady, wake! the azure moon	24
Oh, limpid stream of Tyrus, now I hear	45
Oh! my aged Uncle Arly,	86
Oh, my Geraldine,	66
"Oh, say, what is this fearful, wild,	199
Oh! tell me have you ever seen a red, long-leg'd Flamingo?	201
Oh that my Lungs could bleat like butter'd Pease;	16
Oh that my soul a marrow-bone might seize!	18
Oh! to be wafted away	43
On the Coast of Coromandel	76
On wan dark night on Lac St. Pierre,	116
Once — but no matter when —	155
One, who is not, we see; but one, whom we see not, is;	30
Out on the margin of moonshine land,	63
Owl and the Pussy-Cat went to sea, The	59
Pity now poor Mary Ames,	256
Pobble who has no toes, The	81
Power to thine elbow, thou newest of sciences,	31
Prodiggus reptile! long and skaly kuss!	147
Prope ripam fluvii solus	135
Puer ex Jersey	138
Python I should not advise, — ,A	208
Qui nunc dancere vult modo	137
Quiet home had Parson Gray, A	150

[295]

Index of First Lines

Remembering his taste for blood	205
Rollicking Mastodon lived in Spain, A	125
Roof it has a Lazy Time, The	197
Said Folly to Wisdom,	247
Said the Raggedy Man on a hot afternoon,	220
Sam had spirits naught could check,	254
Selestial apoley which Didest inspire.	146
She hid herself in the *soirée* kettle	60
She played upon her music-box a fancy air by chance,	212
She's all my fancy painted him,	20
Sing for the garish eye,	13
Some like drink	194
Sorry world is sighing now; The	253
Speak gently to the herring and kindly to the calf,	203
Strike the concertina's melancholy string!	107
Sun appeared so smug and bright, The	127
Sun was shining on the sea, The	93
Sun, yon glorious orb of day, The	251
Suppose, you screeve? or go cheap-jack	257
Susan poisoned her grandmother's tea;	254
Sweet maiden of Passamaquoddy,	239
There is a niland on a river lying,	143
There is a river clear and fair,	173
There once was a girl of New York	264
There once was a man who said, "How	263
There once was a person of Benin,	263
There once was an old man of Lyme	263
There's not a spider in the sky,	55
There was a dear lady of Eden,	262
There was a frog swum in the lake,	211
There was a gay damsel of Lynn,	262
There was a little girl,	252

[296]

Index of First Lines

There was a little Guinea-pig,	68
There was a monkey climbed up a tree,	67
There was a princess of Bengal,	264
There was a Russian came over the sea,	238
There was a young lady of Milton,	262
There was a young lady of Niger	268
There was a young lady of Wales,	262
There was a young maid who said, "Why	268
There was a young man of Cohoes,	266
There was a young man who was bitten	264
There was an old man	153
There was an Old Man of Kamschatka	261
There was an Old Man of Leghorn,	261
There was an old man of Thermopylae,	261
There was an old man who said, "Do	263
There was an Old Man who said, "Hush!	261
There was an Old Man who supposed	261
There was an old person of Ware	260
There was an old person of Wick,	260
There was an old person of Woking,	260
There was an old stupid who wrote	264
There was once a man with a beard	260
There were three jovial huntsmen,	70
There were three sailors of Bristol City	114
They went to sea in a sieve, they did;	83
This is the tale that was told to me,	120
This is the Wild Huntsman that shoots the hares;	222
Thothmes, who loved a pyramid,	224
Three children sliding on the ice	69
Thy heart is like some icy lake,	55
'Tis midnight, and the setting sun	26
'Tis sweet to roam when morning's light	25
'Twas after a supper of Norfolk brawn	213

Index of First Lines

'Twas brillig, and the slithy toves	3
Tweedle-dum and Tweedle-dee	74
Twilight twiles in the vernal vale, The	23
Twine then the rays	39
Un marin naufragé (de Doncastre)	266
Un vieux duc (le meilleur des époux)	265
Uncle Simon he	247
Une petite pêche dans un orchard fleurit,	138
Untwine those ringlets! Ev'ry dainty clasp	51
Upon the poop the captain stands,	118
Uprising see the fitful lark	27
We have sailed many months, we have sailed many weeks,	97
We seek to know, and knowing seek;	29
We're all in the dumps,	74
Werther had a love for Charlotte	242
What is the matter with Grandpapa?	247
What lightning shall light it? What thunder shall tell it?	160
What, what, what,	233
When good King Arthur ruled the land,	73
When gooseberries grow on the stem of a daisy,	57
When moonlike ore the hazure seas	49
When nettles in winter bring forth roses red,	186
When sporgles spanned the floreate mead	10
When that Seint George hadde sleyne ye draggon,	267
When the breeze from the bluebottle's blustering blim	14
When the day and the night do meete	241
When the monkey in his madness	210
Where avalanches wail, and green Distress	45
Who, or why, or which, or *what*,	230

Index of First Lines

Why and Wherefore set out one day	36
Woggly bird sat on the whango tree, The	12
Ye muses, pour the pitying tear	148
'You are old, Father William," the young man said,	22
You may lift me up in your arms, lad, and turn my face to the sun,	175
You see this pebble-stone? It's a thing I bought	165